new **vegan baking**

A Modern Approach to Creating Irresistible Sweets for Every Occasion

ana rusu

Creator of Herbs and Roots

PAGE STREET
PUBLISHING CO.

PAGE STREET
PUBLISHING CO.

To everyone who adores sweets.

And to my mom and dad—I love you.

Introduction 6

What to Know Before You Get Baking 9

chocolate & caramel 13

Chocolate Cake with Blackcurrant Jam 14

Dulce de Leche Bundt Cake with
  Chocolate Glaze 17

Chocolate, Chili & Sea Salt Cookies 20

World's Best Raw Caramel Bars 23

Salted Caramel Boston Pie 24

Sticky Date Cake with Toffee &
  Vanilla Ice Cream 27

Fudgy Double Chocolate Brownies 30

Flourless Chocolate Torte with Sticky Ganache 33

Cherry & Chocolate Lamingtons 35

Dark Chocolate Mousse with Spicy Mango 39

fruit 41

Chantilly & Diplomat Cream with
  Tropical Fruit Cake 42

Romanian Plum Dumplings 45

Blackberry & Lavender Ice Cream Sandwiches 46

Light & Fresh Eton Mess 49

Gluten-Free Upside-Down Sour Cherry Cake with
  Crème Anglaise 51

Rustic Peach & Blackberry Galette 55

Perfectly Flaky Mixed Summer Fruit Pie 57

Apple Kataifi with Vegan Whipped Cream 61

Decadent Blueberry Pavlova 62

Crispy & Flaky Dried Fruit Biscuits 65

citrus   67

Lemon Posset Tart with Raspberry and
   Whipped Cream   68

Festive Lime & Coconut Cake   71

Classic Lemon Butter Loaf Cake   74

Orange & Cinnamon Phyllo Cake   77

Lime Cream, Ginger Nuts &
   Cola Gel Verrines   78

Raw Lemon & Thyme Chocolate Bonbons   81

Mango, Lime & Cucumber Ice Pops   82

Bergamot & Olive Oil Yogurt Sorbet   85

Raw Vanilla & Lime Cheesecake Tart   86

Almond & Cornmeal Bundt Cake with
   Orange Syrup   89

spice   91

Chocolate, Cardamom & Tahini Cupcakes   92

Pumpkin Mousse & Cookie Crumb Parfait   95

Crisp & Gooey Gingersnap Cookies   96

Spiced Vegan Honey & Semolina Cake   99

Carrot Cake with Homemade Carrot Jam   101

Star Anise & Pecan Biscotti   105

Saffron Panna Cotta with Rose &
   Raspberry Coulis   106

Wild Berries & Cinnamon Streusel Muffins   109

Matcha Rice Pudding with Blueberry Compote   110

Gluten-Free Pumpkin & White Chocolate
   Oat Bars   113

coffee, nuts & seeds   115

Six-Layer Mocha Cake   116

Heavenly Poppy Seed & Raisin Babka   119

Black Sesame Seed & Matcha Cookies   122

Coffee Parfait with Boba Pearls & Biscotti   125

Pecan & Plum Crescents   126

Coffee, Cinnamon & Walnut Tea Cake   129

Espresso Marzipan Raw Truffles   130

Gluten-Free Poppy Seed Tea Cake with
   Raspberry Cream Cheese Icing   133

Mixed Nuts & Amaranth Snack Bars   134

Rich & Raw Coconut Chocolate Bars   137

booze   139

Caramelized Banana & Irish Cream Cake   140

Strawberry, Prosecco & Lemon Curd Cake   143

Pumpkin & Bourbon Brûlée Tart   146

Raw Apricot, Vanilla & Rum Cake   148

Tarte Tatin with Quince & Cognac   150

Wine-Poached Pears with Cashew Cream
   and Seed Brittle   153

Chestnut & Cardamom Rolls with Rum Syrup   156

Plum & Prosecco Sorbet with
   Crunchy Nougatine   159

Boozy Cherry Truffles   160

Irish Cream & Earl Grey Semifreddo   163

Acknowledgments   164

About the Author   165

Index   166

introduction

It's food that makes you feel revitalized and energetic. Deprivation is not on the menu.

—Diana Henry, *A Change of Appetite: Where Healthy Meets Delicious*

I'll start like this: I love desserts. And baking is one way of finding my peace of mind.

I find cakes and sweets to be a celebratory and important part of a well-lived life, and if you have any dietary considerations or restrictions, you should still be able to indulge in respectable desserts and never be obliged to compromise in delicious texture or flavor.

This book is a collection of exactly those kinds of recipes. They all honor big and bold flavors, without the use of any animal product. But I didn't want these recipes to feel too technical. While I enjoy a good challenge, my aim is to focus on simple ingredients and techniques with minimal effort and impressive outcomes. So, if you're a reluctant home baker, these recipes will empower you to be more confident in your "free-from" baking. Each recipe is carefully written to help you achieve rewarding results. Because I've been there: Looking for the best ways to improve unconventional, vegan recipes that match my taste expectations is not an easy task.

My journey began 10 years ago, when I decided to go vegan. My first months of plant-based eating were a shocking realization of just how important flavor was. I wasn't going to give up on the good food I grew up with, so I immersed myself in the world of food. From the first questionable recipes found on the internet to the elevated plant-based dishes made by trained chefs, I've been following and learning at a constant pace. Running my own plant-based business also taught me tremendous things about people's cravings and preferences, and taking part in Matthew Kenney's culinary academy greatly sharpened my skills.

Growing up in a small city in the northwest of Romania, food was at the heart of my family. My maternal grandmother, Maria, kept an organized and abundant garden until late autumn. There were long vines of grapes climbing the walls of our home, beautifully framing what was then the happiest place I could wish for. She was a master of food and an admirable woman. During holidays, she would make many different kinds of sweets, and on Christmas, there must have been more than ten sweet delicacies on her pantry shelves.

Early on, my grandmother sensed my creative side and welcomed me into her kitchen. I helped her by doing the dishes, kneading or weighing ingredients and eating, of course. While a great amount of that time I was just watching her, to this day I still catch myself remembering bits and pieces—a condiment she would add, her words describing a flavor, a cooking technique or gesture.

Many of my recipes come from those moments. They emulate certain tastes or feelings and I now realize that these memories encouraged me to keep learning about food, so I will never forget them. And for that, I could not be more grateful, and I am forever indebted to her.

My baking style is also a reflection of my life: my travels, readings and forever-growing curiosity. Some recipes in this book are contemporary interpretations of classic ones, while others are unpredictable twists on familiar flavors. This mingling illustrates just how flexible and fun baking can be—even when it's vegan. Whether you avoid eggs, dairy or any milk derivatives, for medical reasons or as an ethical, personal choice, these chapters will take you through some of the beloved classic American treats as well as new and refreshing dishes from Europe.

Rest assured that these well-developed recipes will turn into dishes that uphold the same qualities as their counterparts so they will be equally enjoyed by non-vegans.

These recipes are packed with easy baking tricks and I couldn't be happier to share them with you. For example, basic sparkling water added to a creamed batter will result in a soft, airy and fluffy sponge cake, without the need for any egg whites. A sprinkle of ground almonds into solid doughs will give more butteriness to crusts, while a good splash of alcohol will inhibit the development of the gluten network, resulting in brittle and tender biscuits. Whipped aquafaba (the brine from canned chickpeas) will result in stiff white peaks of meringue that can be used in making mousse or Pavlova. Blending just a few dates with a mixture of various sweeteners and fat will culminate in the most rich and luscious caramel, without any heat.

So, get ready and let these cherished recipes take you on a playful ride. Allow the interesting combinations of flavor and textures to invoke pleasure and curiosity, and let yourself rejoice as much as I do while baking and eating them.

This is a collection of euphoric experiences and I'm sure you will find new favorite desserts in these pages.

Ana Rusu

what to know before you get baking

Before you start baking, I want to make your planning and preparation easier, so here you'll find two sections that will help you master all these vegan sweets. The first section goes over some key ingredients you'll need for the recipes in this book and how to choose the best varieties of each, while the second covers more general baking tips and tricks to get the best results possible.

essential ingredients

Always check the ingredient list of each recipe. For example, some raw cakes require some planning ahead, like hydrating the cashews overnight, so it's better to be well prepared before starting to bake and have everything the recipe calls for on hand.

Aquafaba: This is the viscous water in which any beans are canned. However, for the recipes in this cookbook that call for aquafaba, I recommend you use the leftover liquid from chickpeas specifically, well strained.

Applesauce: You can use whatever brand or type of applesauce you would like for my recipes. If you don't have it in your cupboard, you can also substitute fresh-blended apple puree.

Sweeteners: While this book is packed with recipes that use sweeteners like coconut sugar, agave, vegan honey or stevia, low-glycemic sweeteners are not a focus in my desserts. For those of you who are seeking to control or limit the intake of sucrose for medical reasons, I would not recommend swapping the caster/superfine, confectioners' or brown sugar in a recipe with a liquid sweetener or coconut sugar—the result won't live up to the intended recipe/outcome.

Vegan butter: A 75 percent fat butter is preferred in baking, but if difficult to find, use any vegetable "butter" that contains at least 67 percent fat. Look for the ones made for cooking rather than the ones made for spreading. Vegan buttery sticks from Earth Balance® have 78 percent fat and are great for baking. Naturli'® brand is also good, although harder to find in the United States.

Vegan cooking cream: Any "cream" substitutes that have at least 15 percent fat are perfect to use. I find the soy-based version to work the best. If soy is an allergen for you, go for an oat-based version. Alternatively, you can use vegan whipping cream, which has a much higher fat content and works well in recipes that require cooking cream. Simply use it as a double cream.

Vegan cream cheese: Use a cream cheese that is thick, neutral in taste and stable at room temperature for these recipes. Meggle® brand has the best option I have used so far (although it is not available in the United States). Violife® or Miyoko's® brands have good options, too. For making a drizzle icing, like in my Gluten-Free Poppy Seed Tea Cake with Raspberry Cream Cheese Icing (page 133), you can use softer vegan cream cheese that does not require the latter properties.

Vegan Greek-style yogurt & plain yogurt: Use a neutral-flavored yogurt that is also fairly thick and creamy, similar to a traditional one. Taste before using. If it lacks acidity, add a few drops of lemon juice. I find the Alpro® brand Greek style (any of the soy, oat or coconut based) and Daiya® brand to be good options.

Vegan milk: I like to bake with the "whole" oat milk in these recipes, but pretty much any vegan milk will work in baking. However, I would avoid the rice- or almond-based versions, as they tend to be too watery. I would recommend oat- or soy-based Alpro milk, as well as Oatly®, which is made from oats, or Chobani® brand oat milks. Alternatively, you can use pretty much any soy-based milk, as all of them have a high protein percentage and work great in baking.

Vegan whipped cream: I like the versions that have a neutral flavor, so it does not disturb the other flavors in my recipes and emulates the original ingredients as best as it can. You can choose between ready-whipped versions that are also slightly sweetened, or liquid ones.

Vegan heavy whipping cream from Silk® has a great, natural flavor and works the best in cakes. However, you need to add some sugar and vanilla to it. If the recipe calls for 3.5 ounces (100 g) of whipped cream, simply weigh 3.5 ounces (100 g) of the heavy whipping cream and whip it with caster sugar or confectioners' sugar until stiff peaks form, 5 to 6 minutes. Don't overmix! Or, add 1 tablespoon (12 g) of caster/superfine sugar per ½ cup + 1 tablespoon (100 ml) of heavy whipping cream together with 1 teaspoon of vanilla extract.

how to guarantee the best results

Baking is a delicate culinary art, and requires careful and precise measurements, ingredients and cooking temperatures. Below are some tips to get the best outcome every time.

measurements

Keep in mind that baking requires sharp precision. While all measurements are expressed both in imperial and metric, cup measurements tend to be less accurate, which will result in cakes that sometimes can even fail. So, if you don't own a cooking scale, I strongly recommend you invest in a digital one. The recipes in this book were developed using metric measurements, so for best results, use the metric measurements provided.

For ingredients measured in teaspoons and tablespoons, be sure to use actual measuring spoons for accuracy (and not cutlery).

equipment

Follow the exact equipment specifications in every recipe.

Use a blender for making fine paste or puree and a food processor for crumbly mixtures. For any recipe that calls for a high-speed blender, use a powerful one like Blendtec® or Vitamix®. The twisted jar from Blendtec is a great tool for thick mixtures or nut butters.

Check every pan size before baking and make sure you use the same one described in the recipe. If you use a larger springform pan than stated in a recipe, for example, a cake sponge will result in a much thinner, wide disk that might not be suitable for splitting into two layers. Also, using a bigger pan than required might change the cooking time.

temperature

Always follow the oven temperature stated in the recipes. If you're unsure of your oven, invest in an oven thermometer for greater accuracy.

All temperatures in this cookbook are set with the fan on. Because ovens in the United States do not have a fan, all Fahrenheit temperatures have been adjusted to account for this and are 20 degrees higher than a standard conversion from Celsius.

fold-in technique

If a cake recipe asks you to "fold in" ingredients, use a rubber spatula and carefully fold the mixture around the edges of the bowl and into the middle. Repeat this gesture until just combined and avoid stirring or whisking. The aim is to combine the cake ingredients and trap the air in it, which results in a lighter consistency.

chocolate & caramel

Chocolate and caramel were made for each other, and it's pretty much impossible not to love those two—be it together or apart. This chapter is packed with bold and rich desserts that are so delicious and decadent, you won't even miss the dairy or eggs!

Here, you'll find veganized versions of some beloved classics, carefully developed using ingenious techniques. I recommend you use good-quality dark chocolate in these recipes for more flavor and less sugar.

The Salted Caramel Boston Pie (page 24) will completely surprise you—I used sparkling water as an alternative to whipped eggs to create an airy, fluffy and slightly moist sponge. Got a craving in need of instant gratification? Preheat the oven and those delectable Chocolate, Chili & Sea Salt Cookies (page 20) will get you fixed in no time. As this one is going to get baked many, many times, maybe it's a good idea to add a pink sticky note on the heavenly Chocolate Cake with Blackcurrant Jam recipe (page 14). And if it's too hot to turn on the oven, but you also fancy a rich treat, I think you should look no further than the World's Best Raw Caramel Bars (page 23), which are the definition of pleasure.

chocolate cake with blackcurrant jam

Any chocolate lover will have no choice but to keep this brilliant recipe very close. With three rich and crumbly layers, this cake is frosted with a lush, silky-smooth frosting that has a base of vegan cream cheese and dark chocolate. These two elements are bound together by thin layers of blackcurrant jam. The aim of the jam is to give a slightly acerbic kick and cut through the richness of this indulgent cake. When I'm out of blackcurrant jam, I substitute with a blackberry or raspberry one. And if I feel those are too sweet to cut through the cake, I simply mix in a squeeze of fresh lemon juice.

For an old-fashioned chocolate cake, I sometimes like to skip the jam and keep the cake classic. Whatever your choice, this will greatly impress any guest.

Makes: 8 to 10 servings | Nut-free, soy-free

chocolate sponge

2 cups (240 ml) sweetened oat milk

2 tsp (10 ml) apple cider vinegar

1¼ cups (150 g) all-purpose flour

1 cup (200 g) light brown sugar

¾ cup (60 g) cacao powder

2 tsp (9 g) baking powder

¼ tsp baking soda

¼ sea salt

½ cup (125 ml) sunflower oil

1 tbsp (15 ml) vanilla extract

½ tsp espresso powder

½ tsp almond extract

2 tbsp (30 ml) apple puree

chocolate frosting

¾ cup + 2 tsp (200 ml) vegan cooking cream (see page 10)

9 oz (250 g) vegan dark chocolate, 65% cacao, chopped

¼ tsp espresso powder

8 oz (230 g) vegan cream cheese (see Note)

¾ cup (85 g) confectioners' sugar

1 tsp vanilla extract

To make the Chocolate Sponge, preheat the oven to 370°F (175°C), set an oven rack in the middle position and grease a 7-inch (18-cm) springform pan with vegan butter or neutral oil. Set aside.

In a cup, mix the oat milk and the apple cider vinegar. Let them sit until curdled, about 5 minutes.

In a large bowl, mix the flour, brown sugar, cacao powder, baking powder, baking soda and sea salt. Set aside.

In a separate bowl, mix the oil with the curdled milk, vanilla, espresso powder, almond extract and apple puree. Mix vigorously until combined.

Add the liquid mixture to the dry ingredients and fold until well combined. Pour the batter into the prepared tin and bake for 35 minutes, or until puffed and a toothpick inserted in the center comes out clean. Let it cool in the pan for 5 minutes, then remove it from the pan and transfer it to a wire rack to cool completely.

To make the Chocolate Frosting, place the cooking cream in a saucepan and cook it over medium heat for about 3 minutes, until very hot. Take the pan off the heat, add the chopped chocolate and espresso powder and stir gently until all the chocolate is melted. Let it cool completely.

In a separate bowl, cream the vegan cream cheese with the confectioners' sugar and vanilla, using a wooden spoon.

When the chocolate ganache is completely cooled, add it to the vegan cream cheese mixture and fold it in using a rubber spatula.

(continued)

filling

4 tbsp (60 ml) blackcurrant jam

To split the cake into three layers, measure the height of the cake with a ruler. Divide the number by three to determine the height of each layer. With the ruler, mark the height of the bottom layer with a toothpick. From that toothpick, measure the height of the middle layer and mark with a toothpick. Continue measuring around the cake, inserting toothpicks every few inches. Using the highest set of toothpicks as guides, cut off the top layer of the cake with a long, serrated knife. Carefully set aside. Using the remaining toothpicks as guides, cut off the middle layer and carefully set aside as well. Spread 1 tablespoon (15 ml) of the blackcurrant jam on each layer.

Reserve one-third of the Chocolate Frosting in a bowl for coating, then frost each layer with the remaining Chocolate Frosting. Place the middle layer on the bottom layer, then the top layer on the middle layer and gently press it so every layer sticks well.

Coat the top and sides of the cake with the reserved Chocolate Frosting, using a spatula or an offset spatula.

Refrigerate for 30 minutes before serving. Slice and store any remaining cake covered in the refrigerator for up to 4 days.

note

For this cake, I always use a vegan cream cheese that stays thick when at room temperature. Types dedicated to desserts (unsalted) work best, such as vegan cream cheese from Violife or Miyoko's.

dulce de leche bundt cake with chocolate glaze

Layers of vanilla, chocolate and dulce de leche swirl together into a beautiful cake that impresses with its decadence in this recipe. Who knew a cake with no creamy fillings might feel like a celebration? This super rich and flavorful cake needs nothing more than a luscious dark chocolate glaze and a few sprinkles of flaky sea salt on top.

This cake was inspired by the talented Brian Hart Hoffman's delicious marbled cake, and I spent a couple of weeks developing this vegan version. My goal was to reduce the sugar and fat content of the original recipe without, of course, compromising its remarkable texture and taste. The chocolate on top is a great addition to balance out the sweetness. I'm so attached to this cake.

Makes: 10 servings | Nut-free, soy-free

coconut dulce de leche (see note)

¾ cup (170 ml) full-fat coconut milk

¼ cup (50 g) light brown sugar

2 tbsp (20 g) coconut sugar

⅛ tsp sea salt

bundt cake

½ cup + 1 tbsp (130 g) vegan butter

1 tbsp (15 ml) sunflower oil

1¾ cups (200 g) confectioners' sugar

4 tsp (20 ml) vanilla extract

½ tsp sea salt

1 oz (25 g) vegan dark chocolate, 70% cacao, chopped

1 tsp cocoa powder

1¾ cups (210 g) all-purpose flour, plus more for dusting the pan

1 tsp baking powder

¼ tsp baking soda

¼ tsp xanthan gum (see Notes)

¾ cup + 2 tsp (200 ml) sweetened oat milk

1 tbsp (15 ml) apple cider vinegar

2 oz (60 g) Coconut Dulce de Leche

To make the Coconut Dulce de Leche, place the coconut milk in a saucepan with the brown sugar, coconut sugar and salt. Stir and bring to a boil over high heat. Turn down the heat and simmer on low for 1 hour and 20 minutes, until the sauce is reduced by more than half. The reduced caramel should weigh 2.3 to 2.5 ounces (65 to 70 g).

Transfer the sauce to a bowl and let it cool completely.

While the Coconut Dulce de Leche is simmering, prepare the Bundt Cake. Preheat the oven to 370°F (175°C) and place an oven rack in the middle position. Using a pastry brush, oil the Bundt cake pan with sunflower oil or nonstick cooking spray. Dust it with a bit of flour, shaking off any excess and set aside.

In the bowl of a stand mixer fitted with the paddle attachment, beat the vegan butter with the oil, sugar, vanilla and salt on medium-high speed. Beat the mixture until it is light and fluffy, about 5 minutes, stopping to scrape down the sides of the bowl as needed.

While the butter and sugar are beating, put the chopped chocolate in a medium bowl and set it over a pan of simmering water, stirring until melted. Add the cocoa powder and mix to incorporate. Turn off the heat and transfer the chocolate mixture to a bowl. Set aside to cool slightly, along with the cooked dulce de leche. These two will go into some of the batter in the end, so make sure they are cooled before mixing with the cake batter.

In a separate bowl, mix the flour, baking powder, baking soda and xanthan gum well with a whisk.

In another bowl, mix the oat milk and vinegar. Set aside to curdle for 1 to 2 minutes.

When the butter and sugar mixture is fluffy, take the bowl off the mixer. Add half of the flour mixture and half of the curdled milk. Using a rubber spatula, gently fold the flour into the wet ingredients until barely incorporated. Add the remaining flour and curdled milk and fold again, making sure you don't overbeat the batter.

(continued)

dulce de leche bundt cake with chocolate glaze (continued)

chocolate glaze

5 oz (150 g) vegan dark chocolate, 70% cacao, chopped

1 tsp sea salt flakes

Now it's time to mix the different parts of the batter: divide the batter into three portions. In one bowl of the batter, add in the melted chocolate and stir together. To another bowl of the batter, add in the Coconut Dulce de Leche and stir lightly, until just combined. Be careful not to overmix. The last portion of batter remains as it is.

Using an ice cream scoop or a tablespoon, place three to four rows of chocolate and vanilla batter side-by-side in an alternating pattern on all of the sides of the Bundt cake pan. Add scoops of the dulce de leche batter down the center of the pan. Repeat the process in an alternating pattern until all of the batters are used. Tap the pan lightly on the counter to settle the batters and, using a toothpick, run it through the batter a few times, so the batters swirl together.

Bake the cake for 1 hour, or until a toothpick inserted into the center comes out clean.

Allow the cake to cool for 15 minutes in the pan. Place a serving plate on top of the cake pan and flip it over. Let the cake cool completely on the plate before adding the chocolate glaze.

To make the Chocolate Glaze, put the chopped dark chocolate in a bowl and set it over a pan of simmering water, stirring lightly until completely melted. Pour the glaze over the cooled Bundt cake, then sprinkle with the flaky sea salt. Allow the chocolate to set before slicing.

Keep the Bundt cake covered at room temperature for up to 3 days.

This recipe uses a good amount of fat and sugar and, in this case, the xanthan gum plays the role of eggs; it binds together all the ingredients, resulting in a rich but fluffy crumb.

I recommend making the Coconut Dulce de Leche in advance of when you plan to serve it. You can keep it, refrigerated, for up to 2 weeks. Before using, gently heat the Coconut Dulce de Leche on the stove on low heat so it will become runny again.

chocolate, chili & sea salt cookies

Ever since I cracked the ingredient ratio for making a respectable plant-based version of classic cookies, I've been hooked. And I admit, there's a good reason cookies are loved so much. This version brings all the comfort of a classic chocolate chip cookie with the surprising addition of a little bit of heat from the chili and balance from the sea salt crystals. Whenever I crave something sweet and quick, these are my go-to treats.

The sugar ratio might feel like too much, but for this recipe (as for any cookie recipe where there's science behind it) I recommend following the exact measurements and steps.

For a bakery look and texture, the raw cookie ball dough must nicely collapse when baked, and this is possible thanks to the flour : sweetener : fat ratio.

That being said, have fun in the kitchen—these cookies are super easy and quick to make.

Makes: 18 cookies | Soy-free

⅔ cup (140 g) vegan butter, cubed
1 cup (120 g) confectioners' sugar
1½ tbsp (20 g) muscovado sugar
  (see Notes)
1 tsp vanilla extract
1 cup (120 g) all-purpose flour
⅔ cup (70 g) ground almonds
½ tsp baking powder
¼ tsp baking soda
¼ tsp sea salt
¼ tsp chili flakes (see Notes)
4 oz (110 g) vegan dark chocolate,
  70% cocoa solids, chopped
½ tsp Maldon® sea salt flakes

notes

Muscovado sugar can be found online, or you can substitute dark brown sugar.

Depending on your preferences, use a mild or hot chili variety for the spicy kick or skip it if you're not a spicy food fan. You'll still get a gorgeous classic chocolate chip cookie.

In a saucepan, combine the butter, sugar and muscovado sugar. Cook on low heat, stirring constantly, for 3 to 5 minutes, or until all the sugar has dissolved. Remove the pan from the heat and mix in the vanilla extract. Set aside to cool for 5 minutes.

In a separate bowl, mix the flour together with the ground almonds, baking powder, baking soda, salt and chili flakes.

Pour the butter and sugar mix over the flour mixture. Using a wooden spoon, mix until well combined. Freeze for 10 minutes.

Preheat the oven to 375°F (180°C), and line two baking sheets with parchment paper or silicone mats. Position the racks to divide the oven into thirds.

Remove the dough from the freezer and fold in the chopped dark chocolate, using a rubber spatula. Scoop 1½ tablespoons (30 g) of cookie dough and form into a ball. Each ball should weigh approximately 1 ounce (30 g). Place the balls on the prepared baking sheet, about 2 inches (5 cm) apart (they will spread).

Bake for 10 to 12 minutes, until set, golden on the edges and soft on the inside. Remove the baking sheets from the oven and lift one side of the baking sheet about 4 inches (10 cm), then gently let it drop, so the edges of the cookies set and the insides settle. This technique creates a crisp edge and a gooey center. Sprinkle some sea salt on each cookie.

Let the cookies cool on the baking sheet for a few minutes, then transfer them to a wire rack to cool completely.

Store these chocolate chip cookies in an airtight container, at room temperature, for up to 5 days, or in the freezer for up to 2 months.

world's best raw caramel bars

With the timeless flavor combination of caramel and chocolate, these raw little bars are simply divine. The combination of the various sweeteners and coconut oil results in the most rich and decadent caramel without any heat, and a serving of these will give you an instant boost of vital energy.

Are you surprised to see the mesquite used here? Mesquite powder is made from the dried and ground pods of the mesquite tree, which grows throughout Mexico and the southwestern United States. It has an absolutely delightful flavor and aroma—naturally sweet, slightly nutty with yummy caramel notes. Regardless of its properties, this ingredient is totally optional, so simply omit it if you don't have it.

These are still one of my top favorite desserts after many years of making them. It's no wonder these were also one of the best-selling sweets back in the day when my husband and I ran our food business.

Makes: 9 bars | Raw, gluten-free, soy-free, refined sugar-free

base

2 cups (215 g) raw cashews
½ cup (50 g) coconut flakes
⅔ cup (70 g) coconut flour
1½ tbsp (25 ml) agave nectar
1 tsp vanilla extract
1 tbsp (15 ml) melted cacao butter
1–2 tbsp (15–30 ml) water

caramel layer

½ cup (110 ml) maple syrup
⅓ cup + 1 tbsp (100 ml) agave nectar
⅔ cup (120 g) coconut sugar
3 Medjool dates, pitted
1 tbsp (9 g) mesquite powder, optional
¼ tsp sea salt
2 tsp (10 ml) vanilla extract
1½ cups (125 g) coconut oil, melted

for serving

3.5 oz (100 g) vegan dark chocolate, 85% cacao, melted
2 tsp (12 g) flaky sea salt, optional

Line a 10-inch (25-cm) square pan with cling film.

Place the cashews, coconut flakes and coconut flour in a food processor. Pulse until the mixture forms a fine meal. Add the agave nectar, vanilla, cacao butter and 1 tablespoon (15 ml) of the water. Pulse a few times until the mixture comes together into a fine sticky crumble. Transfer the mixture to the prepared pan and press it down to flatten it into an even layer. Place the pan in the fridge while you're working on the filling.

To make the Caramel Layer, place the maple syrup, agave nectar, coconut sugar, dates, mesquite powder (if using), salt and vanilla in a high-speed blender. Blend until very smooth (a power blender like a Blendtec or Vitamix works best, or if using a regular blender, just pause frequently to scrape down the sides then keep blending). Add the coconut oil and blend again until well incorporated. Pour this layer over the nut base and freeze for at least 4 hours.

When the Caramel Layer is set, drizzle with the melted chocolate and sprinkle with the flaky sea salt (if using). The chocolate will harden right away. Leave at room temperature for 10 to 15 minutes, then slice into nine squares and serve.

These bars will keep in the freezer for up to 1 month in an airtight container.

salted caramel boston pie

I dreamt up this cake when I first stumbled upon the American Boston cream pie, which is basically a gorgeous silky vanilla custard between two layers of sponge and topped with a generous chocolate ganache.

When re-creating my plant-based version, it felt like something was missing. But then I remembered caramel, chocolate and vanilla are made for each other. That's how I came up with the idea of adding the caramel bits into the custard filling. I can't express how excited I was when it came out ten times better than expected. The caramel gets melted into the filling and enriches the cake with some fantastic spots of flavor—it almost works like a caramel syrup.

Not sure which recipe from this book to bake first? Start with this one!

Makes: 8 servings | Nut-free, soy-free

vanilla sponge

¼ cup (50 g) vegan butter, room temperature

3 tbsp (45 ml) sunflower oil

¾ cup (90 g) confectioners' sugar

2 tsp (10 ml) vanilla extract

¼ cup (50 ml) sweetened oat milk

1 tbsp (15 ml) apple cider vinegar

¾ cup (100 g) all-purpose flour

3 tbsp (25 g) fine corn flour

1 tsp baking powder

¼ tsp baking soda

¼ tsp sea salt

¼ cup (60 ml) sparkling water (see Notes)

½ tsp almond extract

caramel bits

¼ cup (60 g) light brown sugar

¼ tsp sea salt

To make the Vanilla Sponge, preheat the oven to 370°F (175°C), set an oven rack in the middle position and grease a 7-inch (18-cm) springform pan with vegan butter.

In a bowl, mix the vegan butter with the oil, confectioners' sugar and vanilla. Whisk until fluffy and creamy. Set aside.

In a separate bowl, mix the oat milk and vinegar and let the mixture curdle for 5 minutes. In another bowl, mix the all-purpose flour, corn flour, baking powder, baking soda and salt.

Pour the sparkling water and almond extract into the curdled milk and give it a stir. Make sure you mix the batter with the sparkling water right before baking (see Notes).

Add one-third of the flour mixture and one-third of the liquid mixture to the creamed butter mixture. Fold in gently, using a rubber spatula, until slightly combined. Repeat the process with the rest of the flour mixture and liquid mixture, adding one-third of each mixture each time. Be careful not to overmix the batter. A few lumps here and there are fine.

Transfer the batter to the prepared springform pan and bake for 20 to 25 minutes, until puffed, golden brown on top and a toothpick inserted in the middle comes out clean. Let the cake cool completely in the pan. Cover with a towel after the first 15 minutes, so the edges get softer.

To make the Caramel Bits, line a baking sheet with parchment paper. Set aside.

Add the light brown sugar to a saucepan over medium heat. Spread the sugar in an even layer in the saucepan and resist the temptation to stir the sugar, as this can cause crystallization. When the sugar starts to dissolve, increase the heat to medium-high and cook for 1 to 3 minutes, until the sugar is amber/dark brown. When done, add the sea salt, mix quickly, then pour the caramel onto the parchment paper in a thin and even layer. Set aside to cool completely. When cool, use a sharp knife to chop the caramel into small bits or break them by hand. Set aside.

(continued)

salted caramel boston pie (continued)

custard filling

1¼ cups (300 ml) sweetened oat milk, divided

¼ cup + 1 tbsp (40 g) cornstarch

3 tbsp (20 g) all-purpose flour

⅔ cup (150 ml) vegan cooking cream (see page 10)

½ cup (105 g) caster/superfine sugar

¼ cup (60 g) light brown sugar

⅛ tsp sea salt

2 tbsp (30 g) vegan butter

2 tsp (10 ml) vanilla extract

1 tsp rum

1.5 oz (45 g) vegan whipped cream

chocolate ganache

⅓ cup (80 ml) sweetened oat milk

3 tbsp (45 ml) vegan cooking cream (see page 10)

5 oz (150 g) vegan dark chocolate, 65% cacao, chopped (see Notes)

2 tsp (12 g) Maldon sea salt flakes

To make the Custard Filling, place the oat milk in a saucepan and reserve 5 tbsp (75 ml) of it in a cup. Add the cornstarch and the all-purpose flour to the reserved milk and mix until the dry ingredients are well dissolved and there are no lumps. Set aside.

Add the cooking cream, sugars and salt to the oat milk in the saucepan and stir. Cook on medium heat for about 5 minutes, until the mixture starts to boil. Turn down the heat to low. Pour the cornstarch mixture into the boiling milk and cook for 10 minutes on low, stirring continuously so it doesn't stick to the bottom of the pan.

When the mixture has thickened, take it off the heat and mix in the vegan butter, vanilla and rum. Stir it well, then put a piece of cling film directly on the custard's surface. Let the mixture cool completely at room temperature. When the custard is completely cool, mix it using a whisk or an electric mixer to make it creamy again. Gently fold in the vegan whipped cream. Refrigerate until you are ready to assemble the cake.

To make the Chocolate Ganache, place the oat milk and cooking cream in a saucepan and cook on medium heat for about 3 minutes, until hot. You can also microwave this for 1 to 2 minutes. Remove from the heat and add the chopped chocolate. Gently stir until all the chocolate is melted. Let the ganache sit for 5 to 7 minutes to slightly cool down.

To split the cake horizontally in half, mark middle points around the side of the cake with toothpicks. Using the toothpicks as a guide, cut through the cake with a long, sharp knife, using a back-and-forth motion.

Place the bottom layer on a serving plate, with the cut side up. Add the Caramel Bits to the custard and fold them in gently. Spread the Custard Filling over the bottom layer. Top it with the remaining layer, cut side down. Spread the Chocolate Ganache over the top of the cake, using an offset spatula or the back of a spoon, letting some glaze drizzle down the sides of the cake. Sprinkle the cake with the sea salt flakes.

Refrigerate, uncovered, for 1 to 2 hours before serving. Slice and enjoy.

This cake will keep well for up to 3 to 4 days in the refrigerator.

notes

The sparkling water in this recipe *cannot* be substituted with still water. Sparkling water reacts with the other ingredients, making the final product aerated and light, similar to a classic sponge baked with whipped eggs. It is important to put the cake in the oven very soon after adding the sparkling water so the ingredients can react and give the sponge a nice, porous structure.

For this cake, I like to use a medium dark chocolate, but depending on your preference, you can use chocolate that is more bitter or sweeter. You can also use a vegan milk chocolate.

sticky date cake with toffee & vanilla ice cream

The very first time I tried an English toffee dessert I was in awe. The rich chocolate cakes I had been faithful to for so long had been easily dethroned. This rich, sticky date cake drowned in the silky caramel sauce, with its beautiful warm–cold contrast, is a dessert that I think few people can say no to. It's a pure, sweet comfort and the perfect finish to any winter meal. For this recipe, use tasty Medjool dates and good quality plant-based vanilla ice cream that uses vanilla bean.

Makes: 9 servings | Soy-free

toffee sauce

⅔ cup (150 g) light brown sugar

¾ cup + 2 tsp (200 ml) vegan cooking cream (see page 10)

⅓ cup (85 g) vegan butter

2 tsp (10 ml) vanilla extract

Pinch of sea salt

date cake

2 tbsp + 1 tsp (15 g) cocoa powder, divided

1⅓ cups (165 g) whole wheat flour

⅓ cup (40 g) ground almonds

1 tsp baking powder

½ tsp baking soda

¼ tsp sea salt

3 tbsp (24 g) ground flaxseeds

¼ cup (60 ml) water

To make the Toffee Sauce, place the light brown sugar in a saucepan and cook on low heat, until the sugar has dissolved, about 2 minutes. Do not stir. When you see patches of melted sugar, slightly shake the pan so the dry sugar mixes with the melted sugar. Be patient with the process of making the sauce. Melted sugar can very easily burn, so it's better to supervise the entire time and work on low heat and with vigilant care. When the sugar starts bubbling and gets slightly darker in color, add the cooking cream and stir. Be careful as the mixture will get very bubbly at this point.

Simmer on low–medium for 1 additional minute. The sauce should look creamy and slightly brown and at this point it will be runny. Turn off the heat and let the sauce cool down and thicken, then add the vegan butter, vanilla and salt and stir until the butter has completely melted. Transfer the Toffee Sauce into a bowl with a pouring spout and set aside to cool. For an easy alternative to making the Toffee Sauce, see the Notes.

To make the Date Cake, preheat the oven to 375°F (180°C), set an oven rack in the middle position and grease an 8-inch (20-cm) square cake pan with vegan butter. Dust with 1 teaspoon of the cocoa powder and set aside.

In a bowl, mix the wheat flour, ground almonds, cocoa powder, baking powder, baking soda and salt. Set aside.

In a small cup, mix the ground flaxseeds with the water and let the mixture sit for at least 5 minutes, until thickened.

(continued)

sticky date cake with toffee & vanilla ice cream (continued)

10 oz (280 g) Medjool dates, pitted

1 cup (250 ml) unsweetened almond milk

½ cup (100 g) vegan butter, softened

¼ cup (60 g) muscovado sugar (see Notes)

1 tsp vanilla extract

2 tsp (10 ml) lemon juice

Vegan vanilla ice cream, for serving

To a high-speed blender, add the pitted dates and almond milk. Blend well until a smooth paste has formed. Add the vegan butter, muscovado sugar, vanilla, lemon juice and flaxseed mixture to the date paste. Blend until well combined.

Pour the date mixture into the flour mixture and incorporate gently, using a spatula. Don't overmix. Pour the batter into the prepared pan and bake for 40 minutes. After the first 25 minutes, lower the temperature to 370°F (175°C) and bake for the remaining 15 minutes, until slightly darker on the edges and a toothpick inserted in the center comes out clean.

Let the cake cool slightly in the pan for 15 to 20 minutes before serving. Slice the cake into rectangles while still warm and place on individual plates. Add one scoop of vegan vanilla ice cream on each slice and drizzle 1 to 3 tablespoons (15 to 45 ml) of Toffee Sauce on top of each serving. Enjoy right away.

notes

Muscovado sugar can be purchased online, or you can substitute dark brown sugar.

An easy alternative method of making the Toffee Sauce is simply cooking the sugar, cream and butter together over medium heat for about 3 minutes, until slightly darker in color. The toffee will thicken when cooled.

If preparing the cake ahead of time, remove the cake from the pan and store in an airtight container. Slice and then warm each piece in the microwave for about 30 seconds before serving. You can also gently warm the Toffee Sauce before using to make it more pourable.

fudgy double chocolate brownies

These brownies are rich, fudgy, bold and flavorful. Skipping the eggs is always challenging in vegan baking, so when a dessert comes out so good in a vegan form, I'm celebrating! These are even more amazing served warm with a scoop of vegan vanilla ice cream—and I kindly advise you to do so (see the Note for my serving suggestion). I'm happy you've stumbled upon these and decided to give them a try. Have fun, and don't forget to let me know how incredible (and addictive) these brownies are!

Makes: 9 brownies | Nut-free, soy-free

8 oz (210 g) vegan dark chocolate, 65% cocoa solids, chopped, divided

½ cup (120 g) vegan butter

1 cup + 2 tbsp (140 g) confectioners' sugar

½ tsp espresso coffee powder

¼ cup (20 g) Dutch cocoa powder

1 tbsp (15 ml) unsweetened oat milk

½ cup (120 g) applesauce

1 tbsp (15 ml) vanilla extract

1 cup (130 g) all-purpose flour

⅛ tsp baking powder

⅛ tsp ground cinnamon

½ tsp salt

½ tsp sea salt flakes

Preheat the oven to 370°F (175°C), set an oven rack in the middle position and line an 8-inch (20-cm) square cake pan with parchment paper.

Set aside 5 ounces (150 g) of the chopped chocolate in a small bowl.

Add the remaining 3 ounces (60 g) of dark chocolate to a saucepan with the butter, sugar, espresso powder, cocoa powder and oat milk. Cook on low heat until all the chocolate and sugar has dissolved, about 5 minutes. Remove the pan from the heat and let the mixture cool for 5 minutes.

Add the applesauce and vanilla extract to the chocolate mixture and mix to combine. Set aside.

In a separate bowl, mix the flour with the baking powder, cinnamon and salt. Pour the cooled chocolate and applesauce mixture into the flour mixture. Stir gently using a rubber spatula, then fold in the reserved chopped chocolate. Mix gently to incorporate.

Pour the batter into the prepared baking pan and smooth the top using the spatula. Sprinkle with the sea salt flakes and bake for 20 to 25 minutes, or until a toothpick comes out with only a few crumbs attached. The brownies should have a slightly creamy and soft center, so keep an eye on these when baking. I recommend testing them with a toothpick after the first 20 minutes to check their crumb.

Cool completely, about 2 hours, before you slice the brownies to give them a chance to settle. They will continue to firm up the longer they are out of the oven. If you prefer a firmer brownie, store them in the fridge and reheat them if serving with vegan ice cream.

These will keep well for up to 3 days, stored in an airtight container at room temperature. They also freeze well: place them in a ziptop bag and freeze them for up to 2 months.

note

These brownies are delicious and fudgy when cold, but my favorite way to serve them is by reheating them in the microwave and serving with a scoop of vegan vanilla ice cream.

flourless chocolate torte with sticky ganache

When developing this recipe, I had two things in mind for it—a dense, gooey texture and a silky, velvety chocolate topping, somewhere between a custard and a melted chocolate, for the perfect decadent pair.

I've been using a breadcrumb cake recipe for a while, and this torte was the perfect time to improve it. I used psyllium husks as a thickener and binding agent, and all the criteria I had in mind were met. This cake is life! It's chocolatey, rich in a simple way, with delightful cocoa and chocolate flavor. It resembles the Italian *panforte* due to its nice dense texture.

Makes: 12 servings | Gluten-free, soy-free

chocolate torte

1 tbsp (5 g) psyllium husks

½ cup + 2 tbsp (150 ml) sweetened oat milk

½ cup (110 g) vegan butter, room temperature

⅓ cup (85 g) light brown sugar

½ cup (85 g) coconut sugar

½ cup (70 g) gluten-free breadcrumbs (see Notes)

⅔ cup (80 g) ground almonds

3 tsp (15 ml) vanilla extract

¼ tsp sea salt

1½ tsp (7 g) baking powder

1 tbsp (5 g) Dutch cocoa powder, plus more for dusting the pan

chocolate ganache

½ cup (130 ml) vegan cooking cream (see page 10), divided

2 tsp (6 g) cornstarch

¼ cup (55 g) light brown sugar

1 tsp vanilla extract

Pinch of sea salt

2 oz (60 g) vegan dark chocolate, 65% cocoa solids, chopped

1 tbsp (17 g) vegan butter

Preheat the oven to 340°F (160°C), set an oven rack in the middle position and grease a 7-inch (18-cm) round cake pan with vegan butter. Dust it with a little bit of cocoa powder. Set aside.

In a small bowl, mix the psyllium husks with the oat milk and set the mixture aside to thicken.

To the bowl of a stand mixer, add the butter, brown sugar and coconut sugar. Cream on medium to high speed for about 5 minutes. The coconut sugar dissolves more slowly in fat than regular sugar, so it's ok if not everything is well dissolved.

Pour the psyllium mixture over the creamed butter. Add the breadcrumbs, ground almonds, vanilla, salt, baking powder and cocoa powder. Mix until well combined. Pour into the prepared pan and bake for 40 minutes until set and slightly puffed. Allow the cake to cool in the pan.

To make the Chocolate Ganache, add the cooking cream to a saucepan and reserve 1 tablespoon (15 ml) in a small cup. Mix the reserved cream with the cornstarch until well combined and set aside.

Add the light brown sugar, vanilla and salt to the saucepan. Stir to combine the ingredients and bring the mixture to a boil on medium heat. When the milk mixture is boiling, turn the heat to low and add the chopped chocolate. Mix it using a wooden spoon, until all the chocolate is melted.

Add the cornstarch mixture and simmer on low for 3 to 5 minutes, until thickened, stirring continuously. Remove the pan from the heat and add the butter. Mix well until the butter is melted. Put a sheet of cling film directly on the surface of the ganache, so it does not form a thick skin. Let the Chocolate Ganache cool in the pan for 15 to 20 minutes.

(continued)

flourless chocolate torte with sticky ganache (continued)

for garnish

Dutch cocoa powder or flaky
  sea salt

To assemble the cake, transfer the torte to a wide serving plate. Whisk the cooled ganache to homogenize it, then pour it on top of the cake. Gently spread it across the surface using an offset spatula. Sprinkle it with cocoa powder or flaky sea salt. You can serve it right away or refrigerate it for 30 minutes before serving.

Keep the cake covered and refrigerated for up to 5 days.

Try adding a handful of fresh raspberries on top of the ganache for a fresh, summery taste.

If you're not gluten intolerant, you can substitute the gluten-free bread-crumbs with classic ones.

cherry & chocolate lamingtons

I grew up eating this cake, called *tăvălita*, but these are actually an iconic Australian dessert that somehow traveled all the way to Romania. Unlike the Australian version, my mom rolled these little cake squares in ground walnuts, but I find the coconut and chocolate pairing to be better.

This recipe uses just a few ingredients and there's nothing complicated in the process. Actually, rolling the cakes in the coconut can be a fun activity to involve little ones at the end.

The addition of sparkling water will replace the whipped eggs and give the sponge a light and airy texture. It is also a seasonless dessert and it will most definitely bring joy to any festive or informal table.

Makes: 20 lamingtons | Nut-free, soy-free

sponge

Vegan butter, for greasing

1½ cups (180 g) all-purpose flour, plus more for dusting the pan

½ cup (70 g) extra fine corn flour

⅔ cup (130 g) caster/superfine sugar

2 tsp (9 g) baking powder

⅛ tsp baking soda

½ tsp sea salt

½ cup + 2 tbsp (150 ml) sweetened oat milk

1 tbsp (15 ml) apple cider vinegar

⅓ cup + 1 tbsp (100 ml) sparkling water

¼ cup (60 ml) sunflower oil

Zest from 1 lemon

2 tsp (10 ml) vanilla extract

7 oz (200 g) sour cherry jam (see Notes)

Preheat the oven to 360°F (170°C), set an oven rack in the middle position and grease an 8 x 10–inch (20 x 25–cm) cake pan with vegan butter. Dust with a little bit of all-purpose flour and set aside.

In a large bowl, mix the all-purpose flour, corn flour, sugar, baking powder, baking soda and salt.

In a separate bowl, mix the oat milk and apple cider vinegar. Set aside to curdle for 1 minute. Add the sparkling water, oil, lemon zest and vanilla to the curdled milk and stir to combine. Pour the liquid mixture into the dry ingredients and gently fold using a rubber spatula. Be careful not to overmix the batter.

Pour the cake batter into the prepared baking pan. Bake for 25 to 30 minutes, or until a toothpick inserted in the center of the sponge comes out clean. Leave the cake to cool in the pan for about 5 minutes then remove the cake from the pan and transfer to a wire rack, with the bottom of the cake facing up, to cool completely. This step will ensure that the top of the cake flattens while it cools.

To split the sponge into two layers, measure the height of the cake and insert two toothpicks at the half-point on all four sides. Using a long, serrated knife, keep your hand on top of the sponge to steady the cake and cut it just above the toothpicks. Gently transfer the top layer by placing both your hands underneath it and moving it onto a clean surface.

Top the bottom sponge with the sour cherry jam and then place the other layer back on top. Using your palm, gently press on the corners and on the middle so everything sticks well. Refrigerate for at least 30 minutes.

Take the cake out of the fridge and place on a clean work surface. Cut into 20 squares. Set aside.

(continued)

cherry & chocolate lamingtons (continued)

chocolate glaze

½ cup (100 g) coconut sugar

¾ cup + 2 tsp (200 ml) filtered water

½ cup + 1 tbsp (30 g) natural cocoa powder

7 oz (200 g) vegan dark chocolate, 65% cocoa solids, chopped

1 cup (200 g) coconut oil

for serving

2½ cups (240 g) coconut flakes

To make the Chocolate Glaze, place the sugar, water and cocoa powder in a saucepan. Bring to a gentle boil then remove the pan from the heat. Add the chopped dark chocolate and coconut oil and mix until the chocolate has melted. Set aside to slightly cool.

Place the coconut flakes in a wide bowl. Line a clean baking tray with parchment paper and set aside.

Gently dip each square into the chocolate icing, using one or two forks, turning carefully to coat all the sides. Allow the chocolate excess to drip off for a few seconds then place in the coconut bowl and coat with the flakes, using a clean fork to help with the coating. Transfer to the prepared tray and allow the chocolate to set.

Lamingtons tend to dry up over time, but they will keep well for up to 3 days, in an airtight container, at room temperature.

To make a variety of lamingtons, use two or three different jams, spreading one-third of the squares with each jam.

Another alternative is to cut off half of the sponge and work with two different styles: one with jam and the other plain, with just the chocolate and coconut coating. To do this, simply use half of the jam and do not split the other half in two layers. They are equally good and it's nice to have different styles on the table.

dark chocolate mousse with spicy mango

This wonderful mousse charms with its strong chocolate flavor and airy texture. It is made with a luscious whipped aquafaba and perfectly emulates the classic mousse texture that is made with whipped egg whites.

Another thing I love about this dessert is the pairing of chocolate with fragrant and perfumed mango, which is absolutely astounding. Just make sure you get well-ripened mangoes and if you can, Alphonso is the best variety to use.

Makes: 4–6 servings | Gluten-free, nut-free, soy-free

chocolate mousse

¼ cup (60 ml) vegan cooking cream (see page 10)

4 oz (110 g) vegan dark chocolate, 85% cacao, chopped

2 tbsp (10 g) cacao powder

2 tbsp + 1 tsp (40 ml) aquafaba (chickpea water)

¼ cup + 2 tbsp (75 g) caster/superfine sugar

⅛ tsp xanthan gum (see Note)

1 tbsp (15 ml) apple cider vinegar

spicy mango

1 ripe mango, pitted and peeled

¼ tsp hot chili flakes

Zest from 1 lime

2 tsp (10 ml) lime juice

2 tsp (10 ml) agave nectar

To a saucepan, add the cooking cream and cook on medium until hot, about 3 minutes.

Remove the pan from the heat and add the chopped chocolate and cacao powder. Stir gently until the chocolate is dissolved. Let the mixture cool completely.

Whisk the aquafaba in a stand mixer fitted with the whisk attachment at high speed for 15 to 20 minutes, or until stiff white peaks have formed. With the mixer running, add the sugar, a few tablespoons at a time, whisking well after each addition, until the sugar granules have dissolved before adding the next batch.

Add the xanthan gum and apple cider vinegar. Mix well, 8 to 10 minutes, until the sugar is incorporated and dissolved and the meringue mixture is thick and super glossy.

When the chocolate mixture is cool, add it to the whipped aquafaba and fold it in gently using a rubber spatula. Spoon the mousse into serving glasses and refrigerate for at least 1 hour to set.

Dice the mango and place it in a bowl. Add the chili flakes, lime zest and juice and agave nectar. Stir and let it sit for 15 minutes at room temperature to allow the mango to be infused with the flavors.

Top the chilled mousse with scoops of the mango mixture and serve right away.

Without adding the mango topping, this chocolate mousse will keep for up to 3 days refrigerated. You can prepare the mango topping right before serving to keep it fresh and fragrant.

 note

Xanthan gum is a water-binding agent and texture modifier used in many foods. It is a food additive derived from fermented sugar and safe to eat raw. In this recipe, the xanthan gum helps thicken and stabilize the air bubbles in the whipped aquafaba and I do **not** recommend you skip it.

fruit

Growing up, I used to go on short family travels around Transylvania quite often. The highlight of the day would be taking a break near a chilly forest and looking for wild strawberries, which weren't that easy to find. If you've never had them, they are a refined version of the classic strawberry, encapsulated in small precious red gems. Their taste is so perfect in their fresh form that I could never bake with them. They truly are a dessert on their own. But I will bake with any other fruit and keep this memory as an inspiration for great taste.

The recipes in this chapter highlight the lively and glowing flavors of natural fruits, inviting you to dive in and delight your taste buds with fleshy, juicy and unpredictable textures. You'll find my favorite techniques for how to make the perfect flaky vegan pie crust and buttery short crust pastry that work as the building blocks in my baking, which you can personalize as you see fit.

Learn how to veganize the popular Decadent Blueberry Pavlova (page 62) using aquafaba—a bean brine with similar properties to egg whites, which wonderfully whisks to high, soft and mesmerizing peaks. The Chantilly & Diplomat Cream with Tropical Fruit Cake (page 42) is a subtle love letter to tropical fruits, best found in winter, while the Romanian Plum Dumplings (page 45) will conquer you with their delicious and rustic simplicity. The Apple Kataifi with Vegan Whipped Cream (page 61) is one of the cakes I learned to make for myself as a teenager because I found it to be better than our traditional apple pie.

Always try baking with fruits that reflect the season, despite the availability of produce all year round.

chantilly & diplomat cream with tropical fruit cake

This is a very popular festive winter cake in Romania. It is simply made with layers of soft vanilla sponge, crème diplomat (which is a crème patisserie or custard lightened with whipped cream), Chantilly cream (sweetened, vanilla-flavored whipped cream) and an array of tropical fruits. This was my preferred cake when I was little; my mother would carefully chop up all the fruits into super small bits, and even took the skin off the pulp of the oranges, which was so important!

Usually decorated with beautiful patterns of sliced fruits, I chose to give this cake a remake and cover it in precious flower petals, which I think conveys the softness and subtle flavors of this classic cake. Isn't it astounding to know how simple yet brilliant a dessert can be?

Makes: 8 servings | Nut-free, soy-free

vanilla sponge
1 batch Salted Caramel Boston Pie Vanilla Sponge (page 24)

vanilla custard
1¼ cups (300 ml) sweetened oat milk, sweetened, divided

⅓ cup (40 g) cornstarch

3 tbsp (20 g) all-purpose flour

⅔ cup (150 ml) vegan cooking cream (see page 10)

½ cup (105 g) caster/superfine sugar

⅛ tsp sea salt

2 tbsp (30 g) vegan butter

2 tsp (10 ml) vanilla extract

2 oz (60 g) vegan whipped cream

4 oz (100 g) mango, peeled and diced

2 oz (50 g) kiwi, peeled and diced

2 oz (50 g) pineapple, peeled and diced

2 oz (50 g) orange, peeled and finely chopped

for serving
4 oz (110 g) vegan sweetened whipped cream

2 tsp (10 ml) vanilla extract

Edible flower petals (or sliced tropical fruits)

Begin by making the Vanilla Sponge from the Salted Caramel Boston Pie recipe on page 24. While the sponge cools, make the custard.

To make the Vanilla Custard, place the oat milk in a saucepan, and reserve 4 to 5 tablespoons (60 to 75 ml) of it in a cup. Add the cornstarch and all-purpose flour to the reserved milk and mix until there are no lumps. Set aside.

To the saucepan, add the vegan cooking cream, sugar and salt and stir. Cook over medium heat for about 5 minutes, until the mixture starts to boil. Turn the heat to low and pour the cornstarch mixture into the boiling milk. Cook for 10 minutes on low, stirring continuously so it doesn't stick to the bottom of the pan. When done, take the pan off the heat and mix in the butter and vanilla. Stir and cover the surface of the custard with cling film. Let the custard cool completely to room temperature.

When cooled, mix the custard using a whisk to make it creamy again. Fold in the vegan whipped cream and mix gently. Squeeze any excess liquids out of the mango, kiwi, pineapple and oranges, then add them to the filling. Gently fold in the fruits and refrigerate until ready to assemble the cake.

Split the vanilla sponge horizontally in half by marking the middle points around the side of the cake with toothpicks. Using the toothpicks as a guide, cut through the cake with a long, sharp knife, using a back-and-forth motion.

On a serving plate, place the clean springform pan that you used for baking the sponge, without its bottom. Line the sides of the springform pan with parchment paper. Place the bottom layer with the cut side up inside the springform pan. Add the custard and fruit filling on top of the layer and spread evenly using a spatula. Add the top half of the cake, cut side down.

Refrigerate for 30 minutes to 1 hour. Remove the pan from the fridge and gently open the springform pan. Lift the springform off the cake and remove the parchment paper on the sides of the cake.

To serve, in a bowl, mix the vegan whipped cream and vanilla. Use an offset spatula to coat the cake with the whipped cream, gently spreading it around the sides. Decorate with flower petals, slice and serve.

This cake will keep well for up to 3 days, covered and refrigerated.

romanian plum dumplings

I really wanted to convey this essential taste of Transylvania while making it seductive for contemporary international palates. My grandmother used to cook these dumplings in late autumn using the ripest plums from our garden, and we were all hooked on them. We ate this as a sweet lunch, as a snack between meals or as a dessert—it didn't matter what time of day. Imagine a soft, gnocchi-like dough that gently hugs a sweet, juicy and fragrant plum. These dumplings get covered in a crisp breadcrumb and sugar coating, mixed with a dash of cinnamon and vanilla. All the tastes are right on point and this dessert should travel around the world and make some taste buds happy.

Makes: 16 servings | Nut-free, soy-free

plum filling

8 fresh and very ripe plums (damsons are best; see Note)

2 tbsp (30 g) light brown sugar

2 tsp (5 g) ground cinnamon

1 tbsp (15 ml) lemon juice

breadcrumb coating

3 tbsp (45 ml) sunflower oil

1¼ cups (150 g) breadcrumbs

⅓ cup (85 g) light brown sugar

2 tsp (5 g) ground vanilla bean powder

2 tsp (5 g) ground cinnamon

dumplings

21 oz (600 g) potatoes, well washed (Yukon Gold or russets)

¼ tsp sea salt, plus more as needed

1 cup (130 g) all-purpose flour, plus more for dusting

½ cup (75 g) semolina flour

1 tbsp (15 g) caster/superfine sugar

1 tsp vanilla extract

2 tsp (6 g) confectioners' sugar, for garnish

note

I love serving these with the Crème Anglaise from the Gluten-Free Upside-Down Sour Cherry Cake with Crème Anglaise (page 51).

To make the Plum Filling, wash the plums and cut them in half. Remove the pits and place the plum halves into a bowl. Add the sugar, cinnamon and lemon juice and mix well. Let sit for about 30 minutes.

To make the Breadcrumb Coating, in a large saucepan, heat the oil over medium heat. Add the breadcrumbs and stir well so the breadcrumbs are well coated. Cook for about 10 minutes, stirring continuously, until the breadcrumbs are slightly dark brown in color. Turn off the heat and add the brown sugar, vanilla powder and cinnamon. Stir well and set aside.

To make the Dumplings, boil the potatoes with the peel on, until fork tender, about 25 minutes then drain them. When they are cool enough to handle, peel them and process through a ricer. Let the riced potatoes cool completely in a bowl.

Meanwhile, place a medium-large pot on the stove, fill it three-quarters with water, add a good pinch of sea salt and bring it to a boil.

When the potatoes are cool, add the flour, semolina, sugar, vanilla and salt. Mix well using a wooden spoon, then briefly knead the batter until the ingredients stick together. Don't overmix. Transfer the dough to a floured work surface. Divide the batter into 16 equal-sized balls.

Strain the excess juice from the plums and keep them near your working space.

Flatten each dough portion to a round disk with well-floured hands and place a plum half in the center of each. Tightly wrap the dough around the plum, sealing the edges and shaping it into a ball. If the edge isn't sticking properly, dip your finger in water and wet the edge to close the dough around the plum. Repeat the process with all the dumpling batter and plums. Place all the dumplings on a floured surface.

Place half of the dumplings in the boiling water. Cook them for 12 to 15 minutes. When they are ready, they should float to the top of the pan. Remove the dumplings with a slotted spoon and transfer them to the pan with the breadcrumbs. Roll the dumplings in the crumbs until they are completely coated. Repeat the boiling and coating process with the remaining dumplings.

Place the remaining breadcrumbs on a wide serving plate and arrange the dumplings on top. Dust with confectioners' sugar and serve hot or cold.

Store the dumplings in an airtight container in the fridge for up to 3 days.

blackberry & lavender ice cream sandwiches

I absolutely love the flavor of lavender and this is one of my preferred ways to use it—combined with blackberry, as these two pair like a dream. Trust me, you will love this pairing too. The tartness of the blackberries cuts through the richness of this creamy cashew ice cream while the lavender gives some floral and woody notes, with a slightly bitter aftertaste. The vanilla cookies give some warmth and sweetness and a chewy, crunchy bite to complete the dessert.

Bonus: This ice cream does not require an ice cream machine, nor any complicated process—it gets its perfect ice cream texture just by freezing.

Makes: 10 sandwiches | Soy-free

blackberry & lavender ice cream

1½ cups (170 g) cashews, soaked overnight

6 oz (160 g) full-fat coconut milk, solids only

⅓ cup (80 ml) agave syrup

¼ cup (60 ml) maple syrup

1 tsp vanilla extract

1 tbsp (15 ml) lemon juice

7 oz (200 g) blackberries, fresh or frozen, divided

¾ tsp dried lavender buds (see Note)

1½ tbsp (20 g) virgin coconut oil

vanilla sugar cookies

⅔ cup (140 g) vegan butter

1 cup + 2 tbsp (140 g) confectioners' sugar

2 tsp (10 ml) vanilla extract

1 cup (120 g) all-purpose flour

⅔ cup (70 g) ground almonds

½ tsp baking powder

¼ tsp baking soda

⅛ tsp sea salt

¼ cup (50 g) caster/superfine sugar, for rolling

note

If you are uncertain about the taste of lavender, use half of the lavender when making this recipe.

In a high-speed blender, process the cashews, coconut milk solids, agave syrup, maple syrup, vanilla extract, lemon juice and half of the blackberries until smooth and creamy. Add the lavender buds and coconut oil and blend again until fully incorporated.

Cut the remaining blackberries in half and add them to the cashew mixture. Fold in the berries using a spatula. Transfer the mixture to an airtight container and place it in the freezer for at least 6 hours, or overnight.

To make the Vanilla Sugar Cookies, combine the butter and confectioners' sugar in a saucepan. Cook on medium-low heat for about 3 minutes, stirring constantly, until all the sugar has dissolved. Take the pan off the heat and mix in the vanilla. Set aside to cool for 5 minutes.

In a separate bowl, mix the all-purpose flour with the ground almonds, baking powder, baking soda and salt. Pour the butter mixture into the flour mixture. Using a wooden spoon, mix until everything is well combined. Place the bowl in the fridge for 15 to 20 minutes to cool.

Meanwhile, preheat the oven to 375°F (180°C), and line two baking sheets with parchment paper or silicone mats. Position the racks to divide the oven into thirds.

Remove the dough from the fridge and divide it into 20 equal pieces. Shape each piece into a ball and roll the balls in the caster/superfine sugar. Place the balls on the prepared baking sheets, about 2 inches (5 cm) apart (they will spread). Bake for 10 to 12 minutes, until set and slightly golden on the edges and soft on the inside. Let the cookies cool on the baking sheet for a few minutes, then transfer them to a wire rack to cool completely.

Remove the ice cream from the freezer and let it sit for 10 minutes at room temperature.

For each ice cream sandwich, place one scoop of the ice cream between two cookies. Gently press the cookies together (the ice cream should spread to the edge of cookies). Enjoy right away!

If you want to save the ice cream sandwiches for later, place them in an airtight container and freeze. They will keep well in the freezer for up to 3 weeks.

light & fresh eton mess

This traditional English summer dessert is a gorgeous and elegant appetizing mess that combines smooth yogurt with tart, aromatic strawberries and crunchy, sweet meringue bites.

Traditionally, Eton mess has whipped cream in it, but I chose to substitute it with my favorite vegan Greek-style yogurt to make it lighter, reduce its sweetness and give it a fresher feeling overall. The strawberries are macerated with a bit of agave syrup and freshly ground black pepper for added heat and surprise. I recommend you don't skip the macerating process: this is basically letting your sliced fruit sit together with the sweetener and get to know each other better. This enhances the flavors and results in fragrant, delicious strawberries.

If you've never made aquafaba meringues before, you'll fall in love with them! I recommend you make the aquafaba meringues a day ahead. These crunchy white jewels require quite a bit of time to whip, and a longer time in the oven, but once cooked, you can safely store them.

Makes: 4–6 servings | Soy-free, nut-free, gluten-free

aquafaba meringues

¼ cup (60 ml) aquafaba
(liquid drained from canned chickpeas; see Notes)

3 tbsp (35 g) caster/superfine sugar

1 tsp vanilla extract

½ tsp lemon juice

Preheat the oven to 285°F (130°C) and place an oven rack in the middle position. Line one large baking sheet with a silicone baking mat or parchment paper.

To make the meringues, whisk the aquafaba in a stand mixer fitted with the whisk attachment at high speed for at least 15 to 20 minutes, until stiff white peaks have formed. After the peaks have formed, keep the mixer running and add the sugar, a tablespoon at a time, whisking well after each addition until the sugar granules have dissolved before adding the next batch. Add the vanilla extract and lemon juice and mix well, 8 to 10 minutes, until all the sugar is incorporated, and the meringue mixture is thick and glossy.

Spoon the mixture into a piping bag fitted with a large piping nozzle and pipe the meringues onto the prepared baking sheet for a neater finish. Leave some space between them as they will expand a bit. Alternatively, spoon small to medium serving spoonfuls of the meringue directly onto the prepared baking sheet.

Bake the meringues for 1 hour 30 minutes to 2 hours until the meringues are set, dry and firm at the bottom. Do not be tempted to increase the oven heat; these vegan meringues collapse when baked at a high temperature. To check if they're ready, simply take one meringue out after 1 hour 30 minutes and let it cool completely. Try to smash it between your fingers. If it's crumbly and completely dry and there are no sticky bits, the meringues are ready. If it still has moisture, cook for an additional 30 minutes. Let the finished meringues cool completely. To keep their crunch, immediately after cooling place the meringues in an airtight container, close the lid and refrigerate.

(continued)

macerated strawberries

2⅓ cups (340 g) fresh strawberries, hulled

¼ cup (30 g) fresh raspberries

2 tbsp (30 ml) agave syrup

1 tbsp (15 ml) lemon juice

¼ tsp freshly ground black pepper

Half of a vanilla bean pod

base

2 cups (500 ml) unsweetened, Greek-style vegan yogurt

To macerate the strawberries, halve or quarter the strawberries into bite-sized pieces. Add the raspberries, agave syrup, lemon juice and freshly ground black pepper and stir to coat the fruits with the agave syrup. Slice the vanilla bean pod lengthwise and scrape the seeds using a sharp knife. Add both the vanilla seeds and the two pods to the strawberries. Mix gently and let the mixture macerate for 15 to 20 minutes at room temperature.

To assemble the Eton mess, spoon a few tablespoons of the vegan yogurt onto serving plates, then top with a couple of macerated strawberries and three meringues (break two of them between your fingers so they are bite sized). Finish with a drizzle of the remaining macerated strawberry juice. See the Notes for other serving options. Keep in mind that the meringues will get soggy if kept too long near humidity, so this is a dessert that should be served right away.

To store the meringues, use the most airtight container you have. They need to be away from any moisture from the air so they can retain their crunch. They will keep well, refrigerated, for up to 1 week.

notes

Due to its ability to mimic functional properties of egg whites in cooking, aquafaba can be used as a direct replacement for them in some cases, including meringues.

This dessert can be plated for an elegant and inviting look, but you can also make this using any type of wide glasses, alternating the layers as you would with a parfait.

gluten-free upside-down sour cherry cake with crème anglaise

With its hybrid, rustic, yet sumptuous look, this soft corn sponge with tangy fruits and custardy cream is a frequent bake in my kitchen. There is something so comforting about the flavor of the earthy corn paired with fragrant sour cherry bites. Easy enough, I like to make this early in the morning and serve it throughout the day. This cake is delicious on its own and if you serve this as a snack cake, you can totally skip the Crème Anglaise. But the silky cream does soothe the acidity of the fruit and round up the overall experience, and I personally very rarely skip it. In terms of temperature, I like to drizzle a slightly warm Crème Anglaise over the cool, refrigerated cake or vice versa.

Makes: 8 servings | Gluten-free, nut-free, soy-free

crème anglaise

¾ cup + 1 tbsp (200 ml) unsweetened oat milk, divided

1 tsp cornstarch

½ cup (110 ml) vegan cooking cream (see page 10)

¼ cup (40 g) caster/superfine sugar

¼ tsp sea salt

1½ tsp (8 ml) vanilla extract

Small pinch of turmeric

sour cherry layer

2 cups (300 g) pitted sour cherries (fresh or frozen; see Notes)

2 tbsp (25 g) light brown sugar

1 tsp lemon juice

gluten-free cake

1 tbsp (20 g) vegan butter, room temperature

¼ cup (60 ml) extra virgin olive oil

¾ cup + 2 tbsp (105 g) confectioners' sugar

2 tsp (10 ml) vanilla extract

Zest from ½ lemon

½ cup + 3 tbsp (85 g) fine corn flour

½ cup (80 g) white rice flour

¾ tsp xanthan gum (see Notes)

1½ tsp (7 g) baking powder

⅛ tsp baking soda

¼ tsp sea salt

¼ cup (60 ml) oat milk, unsweetened

3 tbsp (45 ml) fresh orange juice

To make the Crème Anglaise, combine 1 tablespoon (15 ml) of the oat milk with the cornstarch in a small cup. Mix well and set aside.

In a saucepan, add the remaining ¾ cup (185 ml) of oat milk, the vegan cooking cream, sugar, salt and the cornstarch mixture. Bring to a boil on medium heat, then simmer for 3 minutes on low heat, stirring continuously. Take the pan off the heat and add the vanilla extract and a very small pinch of turmeric. Transfer to a pouring bowl, set aside to cool, then refrigerate before serving.

To prepare the Sour Cherry Layer, preheat the oven to 370°F (175°C) and set an oven rack in the middle position. Line an 7-inch (18-cm) round cake pan with parchment paper and set aside. Place the cherries in the pan, add the sugar and lemon juice and give it a stir. Bake for 15 minutes, until the cherries are juicy and bubbling. Let the cherries cool completely.

While the cherries cool, to make the Gluten-Free Cake, use a wooden spatula to cream the butter with the extra virgin olive oil, sugar, vanilla and lemon zest. Mix it for 1 to 2 minutes, until it starts to get fluffy. It is not necessary for the sugar to be completely dissolved.

In a large bowl, combine the gluten-free flours, xanthan gum, baking powder, baking soda and salt. Mix well.

In a separate bowl, mix the oat milk with the orange juice. Add one-third of the butter mixture and one-third of the milk mixture to the dry ingredients. Gently fold using a rubber spatula. Add the remaining thirds one by one, folding the wet ingredients just enough to combine. Be careful to not overmix the batter.

Pour the batter over the cooled cherries. Spread the batter evenly using a spatula and bake for 25 to 30 minutes. Let it cool in the pan for at least 20 minutes.

(continued)

gluten-free upside-down sour cherry cake with crème anglaise (continued)

To plate the cake, place a wide plate over the cake pan and flip it. Take off the parchment paper and let it cool completely before slicing. Serve with a drizzle of warm or cold Crème Anglaise.

Keep any leftovers refrigerated in an airtight container, for up to 3 days. Crème Anglaise can be made ahead and will keep well, refrigerated in an airtight container, for up to 3 days.

This cake is very versatile in terms of fruits: tangy rhubarb or apricots would be a delightful companion. Or try spiced apples, pears or seedless red grapes for an autumn delight. The farmers' market is your oyster!

Xanthan gum is a gluten-free water-binding agent and texture modifier used in many foods. Xanthan gum is a food additive derived from fermented sugar. In this recipe, the xanthan gum helps thicken and hold the gluten-free baked goods together and prevents the cake from becoming too crumbly. I do **not** recommend skipping this ingredient.

rustic peach & blackberry galette

Baking in the hot summer air doesn't sound very appealing, yet there are a few things I would unflinchingly do it for. One of those is a fruit galette, especially when I find myself with oozingly sweet and overripe fruits on my kitchen table. I think there is no better way of making those fruits shine again than in a crusty, fragrant hand pie. No doubt, part of the magic stands in the nutty, melt-in-your-mouth pastry that beautifully holds and complements the freshness of the fruits.

While I'm very fond of this classic pairing of the sweet peaches and tart blackberries, I also recommend trying other fruits like apricots and raspberries or mirabelles and greengages with loads of vanilla. These small plums have so much flavor potential and pair like a dream in a galette. If you can't find them at your local farmers' market, use regular plums instead. Enjoy it with scoops of vegan vanilla ice cream in the afternoon or, why not, with a dollop of whipped cream in the morning, along with your coffee.

Makes: 8 servings | Soy-free

fruit filling

11 oz (315 g) well-ripened peaches, pitted and thinly sliced (see Notes)

3 tbsp (40 g) light brown sugar

3 tbsp (45 ml) maple syrup

2 tsp (10 ml) vanilla extract

1 tbsp (15 ml) lemon juice

Zest from ½ lemon

¼ tsp almond extract, optional

5 oz (140 g) fresh blackberries

pastry

1⅓ cups (175 g) all-purpose flour

3 tbsp (20 g) ground almonds

⅛ tsp sea salt

2 tbsp (25 g) light brown sugar, divided

⅛ tsp baking soda

½ cup (100 g) virgin coconut oil, cold and solid

2–3 tbsp (30–45 ml) ice-cold water

1 tsp semolina flour

1 tbsp (15 ml) sweetened oat milk

To make the Fruit Filling, add the sliced peaches to a bowl. Add the sugar, maple syrup, vanilla, lemon juice, lemon zest and almond extract (if using). Mix well until the maple syrup is dissolved. Let rest for 10 minutes.

Line a baking sheet with parchment paper. Set aside.

To make the Pastry, add the flour, ground almonds, salt, 1 tablespoon (13 g) of the sugar and the baking soda to a food processor. Using a knife, cut the solid coconut oil into small to medium chunks and add them to the flour mixture. Pulse a few times, until just barely combined. A few bits of solid oil are fine and recommended for a tender crust. Add 2 tablespoons (30 ml) of the ice-cold water and pulse again two to three times. If the dough doesn't come together, add no more than 1 additional tablespoon (15 ml) of water and pulse again a couple of times.

Place the parchment paper from the baking sheet on a work surface and transfer the dough to the parchment. Use your warm hands to bring the dough together and form a disk. Use a rolling pin to flatten the dough onto the parchment paper and shape the dough into a 12-inch (30-cm) disk. Sprinkle the semolina flour on the surface of the disk.

Discard any liquid from the peaches, then place the peaches in the center of the disk, leaving about 2 inches (5 cm) of pastry as a border. Add the blackberries and gently mix them into the peaches. Fold the edges of the pastry over the fruit and make sure all the edges are sealed. Transfer the parchment paper and galette to the sheet pan and refrigerate for at least 15 to 20 minutes.

(continued)

rustic peach & blackberry galette (continued)

for serving
Vegan vanilla ice cream

Meanwhile, preheat the oven to 370°F (175°C) and set an oven rack in the middle position.

Brush the pastry edges with the oat milk and sprinkle them with the reserved tablespoon (12 g) of light brown sugar.

Bake the galette for 20 to 25 minutes, or until the edges of the pastry are golden brown (see Notes).

Let the galette cool for 10 minutes before slicing. Serve the warm galette with vegan vanilla ice cream.

This galette is better served on the same day, but it will keep well for up to 2 days at room temperature, loosely covered with a towel.

 notes

For this recipe, I recommend using very good quality and well-ripened peaches for maximum flavor.

Peaches tend to be drier when cooked (as opposed to apricots, for example). This may cause slight burns on the surface of some peach slices. To avoid that, I like to remove the galette halfway through the baking time and mix the filling gently using a fork, so the peaches on the surface are mixed with the juicier ones at the bottom. To give more glow to the peaches, gently brush the filling at the end of the baking time with 1 to 2 teaspoons (5 to 10 ml) of agave nectar or vegan honey. This step is completely optional and depends on how dry/juicy the peaches are.

perfectly flaky mixed summer fruit pie

Despite my love for rich cakes, I would have a tart, juicy dessert like this over anything else. The lamination of the pie crust requires a bit of patience, but it is a very basic recipe that you can rely on for a variety of dishes. This rough puff pastry method results in an extra flaky crust that you'll love.

As for the fruit filling, I chose a mix that satisfies my need for sour and fragrant tastes: cherries, sour cherries and blueberries, with an accent on cherries. But feel free to add any sweet or tart fruits you love.

The hardest part of this recipe is deciding whether to serve it with vegan whipped cream or ice cream!

Makes: 8–10 servings | Nut-free, soy-free

fruit filling

1.5 lb (675 g) mixed summer fruit (see Note)

½ cup (115 g) light brown sugar

¾ tsp ground cloves

1 tbsp (15 ml) lemon juice

3 tbsp (25 g) cornstarch

1 tsp vanilla extract

homemade vegan butter pie crust

2⅓ cups (300 g) all-purpose flour, plus more for rolling

2 tbsp (20 g) confectioners' sugar

1 tsp sea salt

1 cup (230 g) cold or frozen vegan butter

5–6 tbsp (75–90 ml) ice water

1 tbsp (15 ml) sweetened oat milk

1–2 tsp (4–8 g) caster/superfine sugar

To make the Fruit Filling, toss together the summer fruit, sugar, cloves, lemon juice, cornstarch and vanilla. Refrigerate the mixture while you prepare the dough.

To make the Homemade Vegan Butter Pie Crust, in a large bowl, mix the flour, confectioners' sugar and salt. Grate the vegan butter using the large holes of a box grater right into the flour mixture. Toss the grated butter several times to coat it with the flour and prevent sticking. Add a few tablespoons of the cold water to the flour and butter mixture. Stir using a fork or a wooden spoon. Continue drizzling in the liquid, one tablespoon at a time, until the dough holds its shape.

Transfer the pie dough to a floured work surface. The dough should come together easily but should not feel overly sticky. Using floured hands, fold the dough into itself until the flour is fully incorporated. Form the dough into a ball and divide it in half. Using your hands, flatten each half and wrap each with cling film. Refrigerate for at least 30 minutes.

Roll out both pieces of the chilled dough to about ¼ inch (6 mm) thick, in a rectangular shape. Next, you will laminate the dough. Lamination is the process of folding and rolling the dough over and over to create multiple layers. This step is critical for creating the unique flaky texture of puff pastry. To laminate the dough, fold the dough in half, then in half again, into quarters. Refrigerate the dough for 30 minutes, then repeat this rolling and folding process two more times with each half of the dough, refrigerating for 30 minutes between each repetition and after the last one.

(continued)

perfectly flaky mixed summer fruit pie (continued)

for serving
5 oz (150 g) vegan whipped cream

Meanwhile, preheat the oven to 375°F (180°C), set an oven rack in the middle position and prepare a deep 9-inch (23-cm) pie dish.

Place one of the halves of chilled dough on a floured work surface, leaving the other half in the refrigerator. Roll the dough out into a disk about 12 inches (30 cm) in diameter. Carefully place the dough into the pie dish. Tuck it in with your fingers, making sure it is smooth. Add the prepared fruit filling and spread evenly using a big spoon. Place the pie back in the refrigerator until you work the other half of the dough.

Roll the second half of the dough into a similar circle. Remove the pie from the refrigerator and gently place the second dough onto the top of the filling. Use kitchen scissors to trim the overhang to 1 inch (2.5 cm). Fold the edge of the top piece of dough over then under the edge of the bottom piece of dough, pressing together. Finish the double crust by pressing the edges of the pie with your fingertips. Gently brush the top of the crust with the oat milk and sprinkle with the caster/superfine sugar. Use a sharp knife to cut vents in the top of the pie crust, so the steam can escape while the pie is cooking. Four or five 2-inch (5-cm) slits, arranged in a circle, radiating from the center toward the edges, should be plenty. Use your finger to widen the slits slightly.

Bake the pie for 40 to 50 minutes, or until the top crust is golden brown and the filling juices have been bubbling up around the edges or through the vents for at least 5 minutes.

Remove the pie from the oven and let cool for at least 3 hours before slicing and serving. The filling will be too juicy and runny if the pie is warm when you slice it. Serve with whipped cream and enjoy!

Store the pie at room temperature, loosely covered, for up to 2 days.

You can use frozen or fresh fruit for this recipe.

apple kataifi with vegan whipped cream

This surprising Greek/Turkish-inspired dessert delivers some alluring flavors. When I was a young teenager, this was one of the first proper desserts I learned how to make because it is so easy.

Kataifi is a popular Middle Eastern pastry made with shredded thin pastry dough, which is completely vegan-friendly. The dough is cooked in the apple juices that are released through the baking process, allowing all the tastes and textures to meld. At the very end, a sweet, citrusy syrup gives this dessert more depth, moisture and sweetness. Serve it with the mandatory vegan whipped cream—the fluffy feel of the whipped cream complements the cake in such a gentle way.

Makes: 9 servings | Nut-free, soy-free

maple & citrus syrup
⅔ cup (150 ml) maple syrup
¾ cup + 2 tsp (200 ml) cold water
2 tsp (10 ml) orange juice
Zest from ½ orange
2 tsp (10 ml) vanilla extract

apple kataifi
10 oz (270 g) dry kataifi pastry or durum vermicelli pasta (see Notes)
⅓ cup (70 g) vegan butter, cubed
Pinch of sea salt
28 oz (800 g; 6–7 medium or 3–4 large) apples (see Notes)
3 tbsp (50 g) light brown sugar
2 tsp (10 ml) lemon juice
1 tsp ground cinnamon
⅛ tsp ground cloves
2 tsp (10 ml) vanilla extract

for serving
7 oz (200 g) sweetened vegan whipped cream
1 tsp ground cinnamon

To make the Maple & Citrus Syrup, in a medium bowl mix the maple syrup, cold water, orange juice, orange zest and vanilla well until the maple syrup is dissolved. Set aside.

Preheat the oven to 370°F (175°C), set an oven rack in the middle position and grease an 8-inch (20-cm) square cake pan with vegan butter. Set aside.

To make the cake, break up the kataifi pastry into smaller pieces and set aside. Heat the vegan butter in a large pan and add the pastry or pasta. Cook on medium heat, 7 to 10 minutes, stirring often, until the kataifi or pasta is slightly golden brown in color. Add the salt and mix. Set aside.

Peel, core and grate the apples. The grated apples should weigh approximately 21 ounces (600 g). Place the grated apples in a bowl and mix with the sugar, lemon juice, cinnamon, cloves and vanilla. Set aside.

Divide the kataifi pastry in half. Place half on the bottom of the prepared pan. Add the grated apple filling and use a spatula to gently spread it evenly in the pan. Top with the remaining kataifi and bake for 20 minutes. Remove the pan from the oven, pour the Maple & Citrus Syrup over the cake and cover it with aluminum foil to prevent burning. Bake for another 20 minutes, until the apple filling begins to bubble on the edges. Let cool completely, covered with the foil.

Cut the cake into nine squares and fill a piping bag with your preferred nozzle attached. Decorate each slice with some of the whipped cream. Dust with ground cinnamon and serve cold.

Keep the cake in an airtight container for up to 2 days. Keep the whipped cream refrigerated and top the cake right before serving.

notes

You can find kataifi pastry at any any Greek or Turkish grocery store. If you can't find it, you can substitute it with vermicelli pasta. Use vermicelli that is as thin as possible to ensure a nice, joyful crunch on top.

Use any type of juicy, sweet and tart apples for this recipe, such as Honeycrisp or Jonathan variety.

decadent blueberry pavlova

A Pavlova is a show-stopping meringue dessert and I promise it's easier to make than you think. I managed to stabilize the whipped aquafaba with starch, xanthan gum and acid (apple cider vinegar) and that ensures a nice texture and structure to the baked Pavlova, so I would recommend you don't skip these ingredients. After the aquafaba is whipped, forget about it in the oven for about 2 hours at a low temperature so the Pavlova slowly bakes and dries.

The toppings are very versatile and you can use whatever fruits are in season, but to keep the Pavlova balanced, tangy fruit is recommended. Unlike my Light & Fresh Eton Mess (page 49), I use unsweetened coconut whipped cream (or any vegan unsweetened whipped cream) to top this cake. I also like to cook the blueberries for just a little bit, to get those juices flowing and to help them release more flavor and color. This helps a lot with balancing this sweet and dreamy cake.

Makes: 6 servings | Gluten-free, nut-free, soy-free

aquafaba pavlova

⅔ cup (160 ml) aquafaba (water from canned chickpeas)

¾ cup (150 g) caster/superfine sugar

2 tsp (10 ml) vanilla extract

2 tsp (10 ml) apple cider vinegar

1 tbsp (8 g) cornstarch

¼ tsp xanthan gum (see Note on page 52)

berry topping

¾ cup (180 ml) unsweetened coconut whipped cream

2 tsp (10 ml) vanilla extract

1 cup (130 g) fresh blueberries

3 tbsp (45 ml) lemon juice

¼ cup (30 g) fresh raspberries

notes

This cake is best consumed right after you top it with the yogurt and fruit. Aquafaba Pavlova tends to soak up the moisture from other ingredients and lose its volume very easily.

If you want to make this in advance, simply store the plain Pavlova in an airtight container in the refrigerator. Add the toppings right before serving.

Place the aquafaba in a saucepan and simmer on medium heat until reduced by half, about 15 minutes. Measure the liquid from time to time; the reduced aquafaba should be ⅓ cup (80 ml). Let it cool completely before using.

Preheat the oven to 370°F (175°C), set an oven rack in the middle position and line a baking sheet with parchment paper.

To make the Pavlova, place the reduced and cooled aquafaba in the bowl of a stand mixer and whip for about 15 minutes, until fluffy and stiff white peaks have formed. With the mixer running, add the sugar, a few tablespoons at a time, whisking well after each addition, until the sugar granules have dissolved, before adding the next batch. Add the vanilla, apple cider vinegar, cornstarch and xanthan gum. Whip it for an additional 5 minutes, until everything is well incorporated and the mixture is smooth and very glossy.

Transfer the whipped aquafaba to the middle of the parchment-lined baking sheet. Spread and shape it into a 7-inch (18-cm) disk, creating a crater by making the sides a little higher than the middle. Bake for 40 minutes, then reduce the heat to 285°F (130°C) and bake for another 45 minutes, until the Pavlova is well set and completely dry.

Meanwhile, prepare the Berry Topping. In a bowl, mix the whipped cream and vanilla extract well to combine, then set aside.

Add the blueberries and lemon juice to a saucepan. Mix and mash some of the blueberries with a fork. Cook on high heat for 2 to 3 minutes, until some of the juices are released and the blueberries get more intense in color. Remove the pan from the heat and let the berries cool completely.

To assemble the dessert, place the Pavlova on a serving plate. Spread the vegan whipped cream evenly in the center of the Pavlova. Top it with the cooled blueberries, then decorate with the fresh raspberries. Slice and serve right away (see Notes).

crispy & flaky dried fruit biscuits

These apricot and cranberry biscuits hide some satisfying vivid flavors of citrus in them. Perfectly paired with the crisp, buttery and tender biscuit, the citrus zest comes in to complete the taste of the chewy dried apricot and cranberries.

This recipe is super easy and takes no more than 30 minutes with the resting time included.

I absolutely love to make a big batch of these in the cold months and enjoy them with green jasmine tea, coffee or oat milk. Delightful!

Makes: 14–16 biscuits | Soy-free

⅓ cup (85 g) vegan butter, cubed

½ cup (60 g) confectioners' sugar

1½ tsp (8 ml) vanilla extract

Zest from ¾ lemon

Zest from ½ orange

⅛ tsp sea salt

½ tbsp (8 ml) lemon juice

¾ cup (100 g) all-purpose flour, plus more for rolling

⅓ cup (40 g) ground almonds

⅛ tsp baking soda

⅓ cup (40 g) dried cranberries, finely chopped (see Note)

¼ cup (30 g) dried apricots, finely chopped (see Note)

In a saucepan over medium-low heat, melt the butter and sugar, stirring continuously.

Remove the pan from the heat and add the vanilla, lemon zest, orange zest, salt and lemon juice. Stir the mixture well to combine and set aside.

In a bowl, mix the flour, ground almonds and baking soda. Add the chopped cranberries and apricots and stir them into the flour mixture. Pour the melted butter mixture into the flour mixture, and using a wooden spoon, stir gently, until a dough forms. Cover the bowl with cling film and freeze for about 10 minutes.

Preheat the oven to 340°F (160°C), set an oven rack in the middle position and line a baking sheet with parchment paper.

When the dough is set and hard, take it out and transfer it to a floured workspace. Roll the dough into a 10-inch (25-cm) disk. Using a 2½-inch (6.5-cm) cookie cutter, cut as many biscuits as you can out of the rolled dough. Place each biscuit on the prepared baking sheet. Gather the dough scraps and reroll into a disk and cut more biscuits. It should make 14 to 16 biscuits.

Bake the biscuits for 7 to 8 minutes, until slightly golden on the edges. Keep an eye on them so you don't overbake them. Transfer the biscuits to a wire rack and let them cool completely.

These biscuits will keep well for up to 1 week in an airtight container at room temperature.

note

Other dried fruits, like mango, figs or raisins will work great in this recipe. The dough is wonderful, even plain, as a tender and fragrant citrusy biscuit.

citrus

Citrus has a special place in my kitchen because it boosts any ingredient with an unmatched vivid flavor, yet also stands beautifully on its own. This chapter focuses on bright, zippy and full-bodied sweets and guides you in creating vegan, buttery and moist crumbs without the use of eggs or dairy. Learn how to combine citrus with unique flavors such as olive oil, thyme or cola in vegan desserts that are not only delicious but modern and impressive too.

The breezy Lime Cream, Ginger Nuts & Cola Gel Verrines (page 78) will captivate you with a cola-flavored topping and a lime cream that everyone will remember. For a deeply nostalgic treat, you can upgrade your cake repertoire with my Classic Lemon Butter Loaf Cake (page 74) that has a satisfying crumb and irresistible lemon aroma. Orange & Cinnamon Phyllo Cake (page 77) is here to soothe your sweet cravings in the most satisfying manner—with a custardy texture, this easy phyllo cake delivers a rich Greek-inspired food experience.

lemon posset tart with raspberry and whipped cream

This tart's lemon posset filling is the most delicate, silky and citrusy filling you've ever encountered. The sweet vegan whipped cream, slightly mixed with the tangy raspberries, gives depth to this tart, while the tender, melt-in-your-mouth almond crust complements the soft textures in such a graceful way. I sometimes switch the raspberries with strawberries, peaches or sweet blueberries. Fantastic!

Makes: 8 servings | Soy-free

lemon posset filling

1 cup (250 ml) sweetened oat milk, divided

1 cup (250 ml) vegan cooking cream (see page 10)

½ cup (100 g) caster/superfine sugar

1 tbsp (6 g) lemon zest

Pinch of sea salt

¼ cup (30 g) cornstarch

3 tbsp (45 ml) lemon juice

2 tbsp (30 g) vegan butter

2 tsp (10 ml) vanilla extract

pâte sucrée

1¼ cups (150 g) all-purpose flour, plus more for rolling

½ cup (50 g) ground almonds

¼ cup (25 g) confectioners' sugar

Zest from ¼ lemon

⅛ tsp ground cinnamon

¼ tsp sea salt

⅔ cup (135 g) cold vegan butter, cubed

1 tbsp (15 ml) ice-cold sweetened oat milk

To make the filling, pour the oat milk into a saucepan, reserve 2 tablespoons (30 ml) of it and transfer that to a separate cup. Add the cooking cream, sugar, lemon zest and salt to the oat milk. Bring the mixture to a boil, then turn the heat to low.

Add the cornstarch to the cup with the reserved oat milk and give it a good stir to dissolve the powder. Pour the mixture into the saucepan and mix continuously. Simmer on low to medium heat for about 8 minutes, until thickened. Remove the saucepan from the heat and add the lemon juice, butter and vanilla. Stir to incorporate. To prevent a thick skin from forming on the custard, place a piece of cling film directly on the surface of the custard to cover. Let it cool completely at room temperature.

To make the Pâte Sucrée, add the flour, ground almonds, sugar, lemon zest, cinnamon and salt to a food processor. Pulse a couple of times to mix everything together. Add the cold cubed vegan butter and pulse again, until the mixture resembles a coarse meal. Pour the ice-cold oat milk into the processor and pulse again, until the dough comes together.

Transfer the dough to a floured work surface and use your hands to shape the dough into a rectangular shape. Then, roll it out into an 8 x 16-inch (20 x 40-cm) rectangle and evenly press the dough into a 5 x 14-inch (13 x 35-cm) fluted tart pan. Dip your fingers in flour to help press the dough into the pan if it still feels slightly sticky. Cut off any excess dough, using a sharp knife. Refrigerate for 30 minutes.

Meanwhile, preheat the oven to 370°F (175°C) and set an oven rack in the middle position.

(continued)

lemon posset tart with raspberry and whipped cream (continued)

for serving

4 oz (100 g) vegan whipped cream

1 cup (125 g) fresh raspberries

1 tsp agave syrup

1 tsp lemon juice

When the dough is chilled, take it out and place pie weights (or dried beans) on top. You can use a piece of parchment paper underneath the pie weights (or beans) so it is easier to remove them. This step will prevent the dough from rising in any patches and will help keep it flat. Bake for 15 to 20 minutes, until the edges are lightly golden brown. Remove the pan and check the crust under the pie weights. It should be thoroughly cooked and dry. If there are any moist patches, place the pan back into the oven, without the weights, and bake for an extra 5 to 10 minutes. Remove from the oven and set aside to cool.

Pour the Lemon Posset Filling into the cooled crust and refrigerate for at least 4 hours until completely set, or overnight.

When the tart is set, add the whipped cream on top using a spoon. Spread the whipped cream across the surface, leaving the edges and part of the curd uncovered. In a small bowl, slightly mash the raspberries with a fork. Add the agave syrup and lemon juice and stir to combine. Drizzle the raspberry topping on top of the whipped cream, creating an uneven pattern. Slice and serve.

The lemon posset will keep for up to 3 days, refrigerated.

If you want to make this in advance, don't put the toppings on the lemon posset. Keep the whipped cream and mashed raspberries in separate containers and add them just before serving. This way everything will look fresh and neat.

festive lime & coconut cake

Covered in toasted shredded coconut, this cake has four layers of airy sponges that are harmoniously dressed up with a zingy and vibrant lime custard. I truly can't wait for the cold weather when citrus is in season to make this again and again! This cake is light and delicate yet buttery, fresh and nutty. These joyful attributes of the cake give great satisfaction to any foodie and its elegant and bright appearance makes it ideal for special occasions, birthdays and parties.

Makes: 8 servings | Soy-free

coconut & vanilla sponge

⅔ cup (150 g) vegan butter, room temperature

⅓ cup + 1 tbsp (100 ml) extra virgin olive oil

2¼ cups (270 g) confectioners' sugar

2 tsp (10 ml) vanilla extract

⅞ cup (210 ml) sweetened oat milk

3 tbsp (45 ml) apple cider vinegar

Zest from 1 lemon

2⅓ cups (300 g) all-purpose flour

½ cup (60 g) fine corn flour

⅓ cup (35 g) dried shredded coconut

3 tsp (14 g) baking powder

½ tsp baking soda

¼ tsp sea salt

⅓ cup + 1 tbsp (100 ml) sparkling water (see Note)

Preheat the oven to 375°F (180°C), set an oven rack in the middle position and grease two 7-inch (18-cm) springform pans with vegan butter.

To make the Coconut & Vanilla Sponge, in a medium bowl, whisk the vegan butter with the olive oil, confectioners' sugar and vanilla for 3 to 4 minutes, until fluffy and creamy. Set aside.

In a separate bowl, mix the oat milk, vinegar and lemon zest and let the mixture curdle for 5 minutes.

In another bowl, mix the flours, coconut, baking powder, baking soda and salt.

Pour the sparkling water into the curdled milk and give it a stir. Make sure you mix the batter with the sparkling water mixture right before baking (see Note).

Add one-third of the flour mixture and one-third of the liquid mixture to the creamed butter mixture. Fold in both gently, using a rubber spatula, until slightly combined. Repeat the process until all the ingredients are combined. Be careful not to overmix the batter. A few lumps here and there are fine.

Divide the batter in half and transfer it to the prepared springform pans. Bake for 25 to 30 minutes, until puffed, golden brown on top and a toothpick inserted in the middle comes out clean. Let cool completely in the pan. Cover with a towel after the first 15 minutes, so the edges get softer.

(continued)

festive lime & coconut cake (continued)

lime coconut filling

¾ cup + 2 tsp (200 ml) full-fat coconut milk

⅓ cup + 1 tbsp (100 ml) vegan cooking cream (see page 10)

⅓ cup (80 g) caster/superfine sugar

⅛ tsp sea salt

Zest from 2 limes

¼ cup (35 g) cornstarch

2 tbsp (15 g) all-purpose flour

2½ tbsp (38 ml) lime juice

2 tbsp (25 g) vegan butter

2 tsp (10 ml) vanilla extract

for serving

5 oz (150 g) sweetened vegan whipped cream

3–4 tbsp (17–23 g) dried shredded coconut

Zest from 2 limes

Prepare the Lime Coconut Filling. Add the coconut milk and vegan cooking cream to a saucepan over medium heat. Reserve 4 to 5 tablespoons (60 to 75 ml) of the mixture and place it in a cup. Add the sugar, salt and lime zest to the saucepan and bring the mixture to a gentle boil. Turn the heat down to low. Add the cornstarch and flour to the reserved milk and mix until well combined and there are no lumps. Pour the cornstarch mixture into the boiling milk and simmer on low for 10 minutes, until thickened.

Remove the pan from the heat and add the lime juice, butter and vanilla extract. Mix well until combined. Cover the surface of the custard with cling film and let it cool completely in the saucepan.

Divide each sponge cake into two layers. To split the cake horizontally in half, mark the middle points around the side of the cake with toothpicks. Using the toothpicks as a guide, cut through the cake with a long, sharp knife, using a back-and-forth motion. Repeat the process with the other sponge.

Place one bottom layer, with the cut side up, on a serving plate.

Using a whisk, mix the cooled lime and coconut custard so it becomes creamy. Divide the filling into three equal parts. Spread one part of the filling over the bottom layer of the cake. Top with another layer and repeat the process until you have added all four layers. Gently press down on the top layer, to ensure all layers are sticking well.

Coat the top and sides of the cake with the whipped cream and sprinkle it with the shredded coconut and lime zest. Refrigerate for at least 4 hours before serving.

This cake will keep well refrigerated, covered, for up to 4 days.

The sparkling water in this recipe cannot be substituted with still water. Sparkling water reacts with the other ingredients, making the final product aerated, fluffy and light, similar to a classic sponge baked with whipped eggs. It is important to put the cake in the oven very soon after adding the sparkling water so the ingredients can react and give the sponge a nice, porous structure.

classic lemon butter loaf cake

This bright, zesty and simple cake delivers comfort that I find hard to describe. Lemon may be my all-time favorite ingredient, and it's just fascinating how this floral citrus can give such a deep flavor to any food, be it a sweet or a savory dish.

This lemon loaf cake has a moist and buttery crumb that makes it similar to a rich, classic lemon pound cake, even though it skips the dairy and eggs. Also, I must admit: this is my first choice when it comes to loaf cakes, because what goes better with a nice hot cup of coffee than a good old-fashioned lemon cake?

Makes: 10 servings | Soy-free

½ cup (100 g) vegan butter, cubed and at room temperature

2 oz (65 g) full-fat coconut milk, solids only

1¼ cups (150 g) confectioners' sugar

1 tsp vanilla extract

Zest from 1 lemon

⅓ cup (90 ml) oat milk, unsweetened

2 tbsp (30 ml) lemon juice

½ tbsp (8 ml) apple cider vinegar

1¼ cups (150 g) all-purpose flour, plus more for dusting the pan

2 tsp (9 g) baking powder

¼ tsp baking soda

⅛ tsp sea salt

This cake is perfect on its own and, in my opinion, does not lack an icing. However, if you'd like to add a classic sugar icing, combine ¼ cup (30 g) of confectioners' sugar with 3 to 4 teaspoons (15 to 20 ml) of lemon juice. Drizzle over the cooled lemon loaf and allow it to set before slicing.

Preheat the oven to 375°F (180°C) and set an oven rack in the middle position. Lightly grease an 8 x 4–inch (20 x 10–cm) loaf pan with butter or nonstick cooking spray. Dust with flour, shaking off any excess.

In the bowl of an electric mixer fitted with the paddle attachment, place the vegan butter, coconut milk solids and sugar. Mix on low speed until well blended, then cream the ingredients for 3 to 5 minutes on medium speed, until the mixture is creamy and fluffy and the sugar is dissolved. Add the vanilla and lemon zest. Mix to combine, then set the batter aside.

In a cup, mix the oat milk with the lemon juice and apple cider vinegar. Stir and let the mixture curdle for 1 minute.

In a separate bowl, mix the flour with the baking powder, baking soda and salt. Add half of the flour mixture and half of the curdled milk to the creamed butter and sugar. Using a rubber spatula, gently fold in the dry ingredients a few times. Pour in the rest of the curdled milk and the flour mixture and fold again, using gentle moves, until just combined. Be careful not to overmix the batter.

Scrape the batter into the prepared pan and smooth the top with a spatula. Bake for 35 to 40 minutes. After the first 30 minutes, lower the oven temperature to 360°F (170°C). The cake is done when it is golden brown on top and a toothpick inserted into the center of the cake comes out clean.

Let the loaf cool in the pan for about 10 minutes. Then remove the cake from the pan and cool completely on a wire rack.

Store the loaf in an air-tight container, at room temperature, for up to 5 days. You can also freeze this: slice the cake and wrap it in aluminum foil or baking paper. Place in a freezer-safe container, labeled and dated, for up to 5 months.

orange & cinnamon phyllo cake

Inspired by the traditional Greek *portokalopita*, this cake uses crushed dry phyllo sheets as a base. In her book *Mediterranean Vegetarian Feasts*, Aglaia Kremezi said this cake went viral a few years ago but bakers could not say where the recipe comes from. Her husband (funnily) offered an explanation "A novice, probably frustrated cook who couldn't manage to make a decent pie, ended up with torn-up phyllo pieces and decided to dump them into the batter."

My adapted version of this fragrant and syrupy dessert uses less sugar and oil and results in a custardy cake, similar to the texture of a *canelé*, with alluring scents of orange and cinnamon.

Served hot or cold, this cake is a pure pleasure. You can serve it with a dollop of vegan vanilla ice cream and a mandatory black coffee.

Makes: 9 servings | Nut-free, soy-free

syrup

⅔ cup (150 g) light brown sugar

⅔ cup (150 ml) water

Zest from 1 orange

1½ sticks of cinnamon

phyllo cake

8 oz (200 g) vegan phyllo dough sheets (see Note)

⅓ cup + 1 tbsp (100 ml) full-fat vegan yogurt

⅔ cup (150 ml) fresh orange juice

1½ tbsp (20 ml) vegan cooking cream (see page 10)

3 tbsp (45 ml) sunflower oil

Zest from 1 orange

2 tsp (10 ml) vanilla extract

⅛ tsp sea salt

2 tsp (9 g) baking powder

note

If you use frozen phyllo sheets, make sure you defrost them in the refrigerator overnight. Don't defrost the phyllo sheets on the kitchen counter, as they will become soggy.

In a saucepan, mix the light brown sugar, water, orange zest and cinnamon. Bring the mixture to a boil over medium heat, then simmer for 7 minutes on medium-low. Let cool completely: The syrup should be completely cold before using it in the cake.

While the syrup is cooling, dry the phyllo sheets. Preheat the oven to 370°F (175°C) and set an oven rack in the middle position. Take one phyllo sheet and scrunch it up. Place it on a baking sheet, then repeat the process with each phyllo sheet. Place all the phyllo sheets on the baking tray so the air can circulate between them. Place in the oven and let the sheets dry for 10 minutes, then take the tray out and flip the phyllo sheets over. Bake for an additional 5 to 7 minutes or until dry and super crisp. They should not change the color— if the sheets start browning, reduce the heat to 230°F (100°C).

Crumble the phyllo into small pieces using your hands and set aside in a large bowl.

Adjust the oven temperature to 360°F (170°C), set an oven rack in the middle position and grease an 8-inch (20-cm) square cake pan with vegan butter. Set aside.

In a separate bowl, combine the vegan yogurt with the orange juice, cooking cream, oil, orange zest, vanilla and salt. Stir well to combine.

Just before you're ready to bake, add the baking powder to the liquid mixture and stir well. It will react and almost double in size. Quickly pour it over the crumbled phyllo dough and quickly stir to cover the phyllo, but don't overmix. Transfer this mixture to the prepared baking pan and bake for 25 minutes, until golden brown on the edges. Remove the pan from the oven and pour the cooled syrup over the cake. Let it sit to absorb the liquid, at least 20 minutes.

Slice and serve slightly warm.

Keep the cake refrigerated in an airtight container for up to 5 days.

lime cream, ginger nuts & cola gel verrines

Really, you have to try these ASAP, so I'll keep the intro short. A crunchy layer of chopped nuts spiced with ginger meets a gorgeous layer of lively and green no-bake custard that emanates fresh limes with every bite. Those two are befriended by the most unexpected, yet well-suited topping that resembles the exact flavor of cola for a truly showstopper dessert!

Makes: 4 servings | Raw, gluten-free, soy-free, refined sugar-free

ginger nuts
½ cup (50 g) raw pecans

¼ cup (30 g) oat flour

1 tbsp (6 g) fresh ginger, grated

⅓ cup (50 g) sultanas (golden raisins)

¼ tsp vanilla extract

½ tsp agave syrup

lime cream
1¾ cups (145 g) fresh young coconut meat, chopped

½ cup (60 g) raw cashews, soaked overnight

6 tbsp (90 ml) unsweetened almond milk

¼ cup (65 ml) agave syrup

2 tsp (10 ml) vanilla extract

1 tbsp (15 g) virgin coconut oil

⅓ cup (12 g) fresh spinach leaves

3 tbsp (45 ml) lime juice

2-3 drops lime essential oil, food grade, optional

Zest from 1½ limes

⅛ tsp ground nutmeg

cola gel
¼ cup + 2 tsp (70 ml) agave syrup

Zest from 1½ limes

Zest from ¼ lemon

¼ tsp ground nutmeg

⅛ tsp ground cinnamon

1 tsp vanilla extract

½ tbsp (8 g) virgin coconut oil

Pinch of sea salt

for serving
White currants or blueberries

To make the nut base, place the pecans, oat flour, ginger, sultanas, vanilla and agave syrup in a food processor. Pulse a couple of times, until the nuts are chopped down to about ⅛-inch (3-mm) chunks. Divide into four equal portions and transfer to four serving glasses. Set aside.

To make the Lime Cream, place the coconut meat, cashews, almond milk, agave syrup, vanilla, coconut oil, spinach, lime juice, essential oil (if using), lime zest and nutmeg in a high-speed blender. Blend well until the mixture becomes a smooth cream. Divide equally among the four serving glasses, pouring on top of the nut base. Refrigerate and allow the cream to set for at least 2 hours.

Meanwhile, prepare the Cola Gel. Place the agave syrup, lime zest, lemon zest, nutmeg, cinnamon, vanilla, coconut oil and salt in a clean blender. Blend well until the mixture is a smooth liquid.

Right before serving, divide the cola gel among the serving glasses, on top of the lime cream. Decorate each glass with white currants or blueberries and serve.

note

These verrines are best consumed on the same day; however, if you want to make them ahead, keep everything refrigerated and spoon the cola gel over the lime cream right before serving. This way you will avoid the gel seeping through the lime cream and making the crumble too moist.

raw lemon & thyme chocolate bonbons

Here is a celebration of my all-time favorite ingredients: chocolate and lemon. These cute bonbons are coated in a raw, tempered chocolate; if you've ever wondered how chocolate can get so shiny and crisp, it's because of the tempering process. A food thermometer is needed to monitor the temperature of your melted chocolate and it does take a bit of patience, yet be sure that this is totally worth it. It will give the final product a smooth and glossy finish and it keeps it from easily melting in your fingers.

To spice things up even more, I added some chopped fresh thyme—herbs are a great addition to chocolate and lemon, giving them some extra earthy and floral notes. These cute bonbons are a fun and elegant treat to make and share with any chocolate lover.

Makes: 35 bonbons | Raw, gluten-free, soy-free, refined sugar-free

lemon & thyme filling

¾ cup (80 g) raw cashews

½ cup + 1 tbsp (140 ml) agave nectar

3 tbsp (45 ml) lemon juice

Zest from 1½ lemons

2 tsp (10 ml) vanilla extract

Small pinch of sea salt

½ cup (50 g) coconut flour

⅓ cup (70 g) virgin coconut oil

1 tbsp (2 g) fresh lemon thyme, minced

tempered chocolate

⅓ cup (80 g) cacao butter, cut into pieces

¾ cup (60 g) cacao powder

2 tbsp (20 g) fine powdered coconut sugar or powdered cane sugar

Vanilla seeds from ⅓ bean

Small pinch of sea salt

for serving

Zest from 1 lemon

Line a baking tray with parchment paper and set aside.

To make the filling, add the cashews, agave nectar, lemon juice, lemon zest, vanilla and salt to a high-speed blender. Blend well, until very smooth and creamy. Add the coconut flour and coconut oil and blend to incorporate. Add the minced thyme and stir with a spatula to combine. Transfer the mixture to a wide plate and refrigerate for an hour, or until hard enough to handle.

When ready to make the bonbons, measure 0.3 ounce (10 g) of filling and shape it into a ball. Repeat this process with the remaining filling. The mixture should make approximately 35 balls. Place the balls on the parchment-lined tray and refrigerate again for 30 minutes.

While the bonbons are chilling, melt the cacao butter using a double boiler. If you don't have a double boiler, place a pot half filled with water on the stove and bring to a boil on a medium heat. On top of the pot, place a clean heatproof bowl that is large enough to fit in the pot. The bowl should not touch the boiling water. This technique is also called *bain-marie* and it is used for transmitting a gentle heat. Add the cacao butter to the bowl and mix from time to time until the cacao butter is completely melted. Add the cacao powder, sugar, vanilla and salt. Stir well to combine. Using a food thermometer, test the melted mixture. When the mixture reaches 115°F (46°C), remove the pan from the heat. Cool the mixture to 82°F (28°C), stirring to help the cooling process. When the mixture cools to 82°F (28°C), return the pan to the heat, and reheat until the mixture reaches 88°F (31°C), then remove the pan from the heat.

Now you can coat the bonbons. Dip the bonbons in the melted chocolate, using a fork. Return them to the parchment-lined baking tray and allow them to set at room temperature for 10 minutes. Sprinkle with the fresh grated lemon zest, then refrigerate for at least 1 hour to set.

Store the bonbons for up to 7 days refrigerated in an airtight container.

If you want to skip the tempering process, simply substitute 5 ounces (150 g) of vegan dark chocolate. Chop and melt the chocolate on a double boiler, then follow the dipping process.

mango, lime & cucumber ice pops

Pull out those popsicle molds and sticks! Made with just a few ingredients, this dessert blends raw mango and fragrant limes, then spices them with a couple of drops of essential peppermint oil for a breezy feel. It's an invigorating treat that pairs divinely with hot summer weather. These little ice pops deliver great satisfaction: they are sweet and tart, super fragrant and refreshing.

For a summer night dessert, I like to skip the peppermint and add a splash of gin, and make it an "adults-only" fun sorbet to share with friends. The best idea, I would say.

Makes: 6–8 ice pops | Raw, soy-free, nut-free, gluten-free, refined sugar-free

2¼ cups (300 g) ripe mango, pitted and cubed

½ cup (100 g) cucumber, peeled and diced

½ cup (110 ml) agave syrup (or vegan honey)

¼ cup (50 ml) lime juice

1 tbsp (6 g) lime zest

¼ tsp vanilla extract

2–3 drops peppermint essential oil, food grade (see Notes)

Pinch of sea salt

Place the cubed mango, cucumber, agave syrup, lime juice, lime zest, vanilla, peppermint and sea salt in a blender. Blend until silky smooth.

Pour the mixture into six to eight popsicle molds (depending on the size of your molds) and insert the popsicle sticks. Freeze for at least 6 hours until the pop is frozen solid. Alternatively, freeze overnight.

Defrost for about 5 minutes before taking the pops out so they come out whole.

These ice pops will keep for up to 4 weeks in the freezer. Just make sure you put them in a ziptop bag to ensure their flavor.

 notes

You can use fresh mint leaves instead of peppermint essential oil. Simply substitute the essential oil with 8 to 10 fresh mint leaves.

You can also make this recipe into a sorbet. Simply skip the popsicle molds and freeze in an airtight container and follow the freezing steps for my Plum & Prosecco Sorbet with Crunchy Nougatine recipe on page 159.

bergamot & olive oil yogurt sorbet

This lovely bergamot and olive oil sorbet is just the right dessert you'd need on a sweltering summer day. With a slightly bitter kick from the bergamot juice, this dessert is sweet and tangy and becomes even better with a good drizzle of the punchy and peppery olive oil on top, which I never skip! And don't worry if you don't own an ice cream machine—you won't need one. This is a light and fragrant frozen treat that you can also make into fun ice pops.

Makes: 4 servings | Gluten-free, nut-free, soy-free, refined sugar-free

2 cups (500 ml) vegan plain Greek-style yogurt

⅔ cup (160 ml) agave nectar

2 tsp (10 ml) vanilla extract

1½ tbsp (23 ml) bergamot juice

Zest from ½ lemon

Pinch of sea salt

2–4 tbsp (30–60 ml) extra virgin olive oil

In a bowl, whisk the vegan yogurt, agave nectar, vanilla, bergamot juice, lemon zest and salt vigorously until well mixed. Place the mixture in an ice cream maker and process according to the manufacturer's instructions. Transfer to an airtight container and freeze for at least 2 hours.

If you don't have an ice cream machine, pour the yogurt into an airtight container, close the lid and freeze. After 2 to 3 hours, take the mixture out of the freezer and transfer to a blender. Blend well until creamy, to prevent any ice crystals forming during the freezing process. Transfer back to the container and freeze again for up to 4 hours or overnight. This technique will help break down any ice crystals that formed and will give the sorbet a more soft/creamy texture.

Before serving, let the sorbet sit for 5 minutes at room temperature. Scoop and serve with a good drizzle of olive oil and enjoy!

This frozen yogurt sorbet will keep for up to 4 weeks in the freezer, stored in an airtight container.

Bergamot is a wonderful citrus grown in Italy, France or Turkey and its taste is a mix between a lemon and a yellow grapefruit, but more bitter, with a distinctive scent. Not sure where to find it? No worries, you can simply substitute the bergamot juice with lemon juice and add 2 to 3 drops of bergamot essential oil, which is much more easily found in Whole Foods® or any health food markets.

raw vanilla & lime cheesecake tart

This cheesecake features a classic combo of tartness and richness that always hits the right spot. Having limes center stage, this tart is a celebration of summer and freshness. It's perfumed, delightful and its silky-smooth texture makes you go for a second slice. The gluten-free, dairy-free hazelnut base is spiced with a pinch of ginger—a great pair for limes—and the topping has a sharp and zingy taste that balances the sweet vanilla layer so well. The number of limes used in this recipe will ensure an impressive, lip-smacking flavor. Save some of this topping in a sauce cup, so your guests can add an extra kick to their slices. And don't forget to soak your cashews for the topping the night before making this!

Makes: 8 servings | Raw, gluten-free, soy-free, refined-sugar free

hazelnut crust

¾ cup (90 g) raw hazelnuts

½ cup (40 g) oat flour

1½ tsp (3 g) ground ginger powder

1½ tbsp (23 ml) maple syrup

Pinch of sea salt

vanilla–lime filling

1¾ cups (200 g) raw cashews, soaked overnight

¼ cup (60 ml) ice-cold water

3½ tbsp (52 ml) lemon juice

¼ cup (50 ml) agave nectar

1 tsp nutritional yeast, optional

2½ tbsp (35 g) coconut oil

1½ tsp (8 ml) vanilla extract

Pinch of sea salt

Zest from 1 organic lime

lime topping (see note)

3 tbsp (20 g) raw cashews, soaked overnight

1½ tbsp (20 ml) agave nectar

½ cup (10 g) fresh spinach leaves

1 tbsp (15 ml) lime juice

1 tsp lemon juice

2 tsp (10 ml) vanilla extract

Zest from 1 lime

⅛ tsp ground nutmeg

1½ tbsp (23 ml) water

Pinch of sea salt

garnish

Zest from 1 lime

Release the bottom disk of a 7-inch (18-cm) fluted tart pan with a removable bottom. Lay a piece of cling film over the bottom, covering its surface entirely. Secure the ring back onto the disk. Set aside.

To make the crust, place the hazelnuts and oat flour in a food processor and process until a fine meal is achieved. Add the ginger, maple syrup and salt and blend until the mixture clumps together easily when you pinch it with your fingers. Place the crust mixture in the prepared tart pan and press down with a spatula, to form an even layer across the bottom and sides of the pan. Set aside.

To make the Vanilla–Lime Filling, drain the cashews and add them to a high-speed blender. Add the water and lemon juice and blend until smooth and silky. Add the agave nectar, nutritional yeast, coconut oil, vanilla and sea salt and blend again to combine. Add the lime zest and mix well using a spoon. Pour the filling into the hazelnut crust. Spread evenly using a spatula. Place the cake in the freezer for at least 6 hours or overnight.

To make the topping, drain the cashews. Add them to a high-speed blender along with the agave, spinach, lime and lemon juice, vanilla, lime zest, ground nutmeg, water and salt. Blend well until smooth and creamy. Pour the mixture into a bowl and refrigerate until ready to use.

When the lime cheesecake is set, remove it from the freezer and refrigerate for 30 minutes to slowly defrost. Pour the topping over the cheesecake and level it with an offset spatula. Garnish with the some of the lime zest.

Slice the cheesecake and serve right away, keeping the remaining lime topping on the table for anyone who wants some extra zing on the cheese-cake.

Keep the lime tart in the freezer, in an airtight container, for up to 3 weeks.

note

The lime topping can be made ahead and refrigerated for up to 3 days.

almond & cornmeal bundt cake with orange syrup

With its bright and zesty orange flavor, this Bundt cake is a winter celebration! This cake uses a whole, boiled and blended orange, and together with the coarse polenta, it gives the cake a lovely custardy and tender texture. It makes such a good pair with the sticky syrup, and I also love serving it with a dollop of vegan whipped cream!

A piece of advice for this recipe is to pick the right orange. It's important to use an organic one that is safe to consume with the peel on. Taste the orange after boiling and make sure the bitterness has gone away. If the peel is still bitter, boil for another 30 minutes.

Makes: 9 servings | Soy-free

orange syrup
½ cup (110 ml) orange juice
3 tbsp (40 g) light brown sugar
2 tsp (10 ml) vanilla extract

almond & cornmeal cake
1 medium organic orange
½ cup (50 g) ground almonds
⅓ cup (40 g) all-purpose flour
⅔ cup (75 g) cornmeal
2 tsp (9 g) baking powder
¼ tsp ground cardamom
Pinch of sea salt
½ cup (130 ml) unsweetened oat milk
⅓ cup (85 g) light brown sugar
¼ cup (50 ml) sunflower oil
2 tsp (10 ml) vanilla extract
1 tsp lemon zest

To make the Orange Syrup, place the orange juice and sugar in a saucepan. Bring to a boil over medium heat, then reduce to a gentle simmer and cook for 5 to 7 minutes, or until the syrup starts to thicken. Stir in the vanilla, then set aside to cool completely.

To make the cake, place the orange in a pan and add water until the orange begins to float. Bring the water to a boil, then reduce the heat to a gentle boil and place a lid on the pan. Cook for 1 hour and 30 minutes. Check the skin; if the peel is still bitter, boil for another 30 minutes. Remove the orange from the pan, cut into quarters and remove any seeds. Allow the orange to cool for 10 minutes, then add to a blender and blitz to form a smooth paste. Set aside.

Preheat the oven to 375°F (180°C) and set an oven rack in the middle position. Grease a non-stick Bundt cake pan with cooking spray and set aside.

Place the ground almonds, flour, cornmeal, baking powder, cardamom and salt in a bowl. Mix and set aside.

In a separate bowl, mix the oat milk, sugar, oil, vanilla, lemon zest and blended orange paste well, then let the mixture sit for 3 to 5 minutes to rest, until the sugar is almost dissolved. Pour the wet ingredients over the flour mixture and mix gently with a rubber spatula.

Pour the batter into the prepared Bundt tin. Bake for 30 minutes, or until golden brown on top and a toothpick inserted into the center of the cake comes out clean. Remove the pan from the oven and immediately drizzle half of the cold syrup over the cake, using a spoon. Let it sit for about 10 minutes, until the cake absorbs the liquid and has cooled slightly.

Invert the cake onto a serving plate and brush the top and sides of the cake with the remaining syrup. Allow the cake to cool slightly before serving, or serve when barely warm.

Keep the cake in an airtight container, at room temperature or in the refrigerator, for up to 4 days.

spice

This chapter celebrates the expressivity of spices. It covers a tiny part of the multitude of spices that we have access to, but every single recipe here is a statement of uniqueness. You will learn some distinguished pairings and how to blend flavors in your vegan baking so that the taste is never smothered or irritating, but enhanced and balanced for a delicious result.

These recipes are bursting with warm and woody scents as well as floral and elegant ones.

Inspired by a traditional Romanian dessert, the Spiced Vegan Honey & Semolina Cake (page 99) is a vegan snack that will fascinate with gentle flavors of honey and vanilla. If you are looking for a modern way of serving pumpkin pie, I think you should try the Pumpkin Mousse & Cookie Crumb Parfait (page 95), which conveys the homey flavors of the traditional American pie so well.

There is something for any taste here and this chapter will certainly put you in the baking mood.

chocolate, cardamom & tahini cupcakes

With a nice crumb and a delicious buttercream, these cupcakes are little pieces of heaven. To cut the fattiness of the buttercream, I added classic plant-based cream cheese and it works wonders with tahini. The combination of chocolate, cardamom and sesame is one that shouldn't be missed.

Makes: 12 cupcakes | Nut-free, soy-free

chocolate cupcakes

1¼ cups (150 g) all-purpose flour

1 cup (200 g) light brown sugar

¾ cup (60 g) cocoa powder

2 tsp (10 ml) vanilla extract

½ tsp ground cardamom

¼ tsp ground cinnamon

¼ tsp espresso powder

1 tsp baking powder

¼ tsp baking soda

⅛ tsp sea salt

1 cup (240 ml) sweetened oat milk

1 tsp apple cider vinegar

½ cup (125 ml) sunflower oil

2 tbsp (32 g) unsweetened applesauce

tahini buttercream

½ cup (100 g) light brown sugar

½ cup (100 g) vegan butter, cubed and at room temperature

¼ cup (50 ml) tahini paste

½ tsp vanilla extract

¼ tsp ground cardamom

1 tbsp (15 ml) vegan cooking cream (see page 10), plus more if needed

Pinch of sea salt

for serving

1 tbsp (11 g) cocoa nibs

1–2 tsp (2–4 g) mixed white and black sesame seeds

Preheat the oven to 370°F (175°C) and set an oven rack in the middle position. Place cupcake liners in a standard muffin tin.

To make the cupcakes, place the flour, sugar, cocoa powder, vanilla, cardamom, cinnamon, espresso powder, baking powder, baking soda and salt in a medium bowl. Mix well to combine.

In a separate bowl, mix the oat milk, vinegar, oil and applesauce. Whisk to combine.

Pour the liquid mixture into the dry ingredients and fold in the flour until just combined.

Pour the batter into muffin tins, filling two-thirds of the cup. Bake for 18 to 20 minutes, or until a toothpick inserted into the middle comes out clean. Remove the cupcakes from the oven and cool for 2 minutes, then use a fork to help transfer the muffins to a cooling rack. Cool completely.

While the cupcakes cool, to make the Tahini Buttercream, place the sugar in a blender and blend until very fine, similar to the texture of confectioners' sugar. In the bowl of a stand mixer, beat the vegan butter and tahini until well combined and creamy. Add the blended sugar and continue beating. Add the vanilla, cardamom, vegan cooking cream and salt. Beat until smooth and fluffy, about 5 minutes, adding an additional teaspoon of cooking cream, if needed. When ready, transfer the buttercream to a piping bag with your preferred nozzle and set aside.

To assemble the cupcakes, place the cooled cupcakes on a wide serving plate and decorate each cupcake with the Tahini Buttercream. Sprinkle the tops with the cocoa nibs and sesame seeds and serve.

The cupcakes will keep for up to 3 days, refrigerated in an airtight container.

pumpkin mousse & cookie crumb parfait

I have a passion for desserts in a glass. It gets a bit messy when I'm doing them, but they are very easy to make. This one looks (and tastes) irresistible and what I love the most is the many textures it has and the satisfying feeling at the end. The layers of pumpkin are gently spiced and the whipped cream balances the flavor, while the cookie crumb and pecans give an extra dimension to this creamy, dreamy dessert. To save some time, I recommend you have the Crisp & Gooey Gingersnap Cookies (page 96) baked beforehand, but nonetheless they are super easy to make.

Makes: 6 parfaits | Soy-free

pumpkin custard

½ cup (120 ml) vegan cooking cream (see page 10)

2 cups + 3 tbsp (520 ml) sweetened oat milk, divided

¼ cup (60 ml) agave nectar

¼ tsp sea salt

2 tbsp (15 g) cornstarch

11 oz (300 g) pumpkin puree

2 tsp (10 ml) vanilla extract

½ tsp ground cinnamon

½ tsp ground cloves

¼ tsp ground nutmeg

pumpkin mousse

4 oz (100 g) vegan whipped cream, sweetened

2 tsp (10 ml) lemon juice

other layers

½ batch of Crisp & Gooey Gingersnap Cookies (page 96)

⅔ cup (60 g) toasted pecans, chopped

3 oz (75 g) sweetened vegan whipped cream

To make the Pumpkin Custard, place the cooking cream, 2 cups (480 ml) of the oat milk, the agave nectar and salt in a saucepan. Bring the mixture to a boil over medium heat. Turn the heat to low. In a small cup, mix the cornstarch with the remaining 3 tablespoons (40 ml) of the milk until the cornstarch is dissolved. Add the cornstarch blend to the boiling milk mixture. Using a whisk, stir continuously to avoid lumps. Cook on low to medium, stirring constantly, for 4 to 5 minutes, until thickened. Add the pumpkin puree, vanilla, cinnamon, cloves and nutmeg, and mix well to combine. Cook for 1 to 2 more minutes then remove from the heat.

Cover the surface of the Pumpkin Custard with cling film and allow it to cool completely at room temperature.

To make the Pumpkin Mousse, add the whipped cream and lemon juice to a bowl and mix to combine. Measure 11 ounces (300 g) of the cooled Pumpkin Custard and add it to the whipped cream. Keep the rest for layering. Gently fold the Pumpkin Custard into the whipped cream, using a spatula. Transfer the mousse into a piping bag and place it in the fridge until ready to plate. Alternatively, you can leave it in the bowl and scoop it with a spoon when assembling the parfaits.

To make the cookie crumble, place the Gingersnap Cookies in a food processor. Process until a biscuit crumb forms, no more than a few seconds. A few larger pieces are welcome for more texture.

Take six serving glasses and add 1 to 2 tablespoons (7 to 14 g) of the cookie crumble to the bottom of each glass. Add 1 to 2 tablespoons (15 to 30 ml) of the Pumpkin Mousse to each glass, followed by a layer of about 1 tablespoon (15 ml) of the Pumpkin Custard in each glass. Sprinkle with the chopped pecans and more cookie crumble and add a dollop of the whipped cream to each glass. Finally, top with the remaining Pumpkin Mousse.

Refrigerate for 15 minutes and finish with any remaining crumble and pecans, just before serving, to keep them crunchy.

note

The Pumpkin Custard, Mousse and whipped cream will keep well for up to 3 days, refrigerated, in airtight containers. When ready to serve, assemble the parfait in glasses. Keep the cookie crumble and nuts at room temperature.

crisp & gooey gingersnap cookies

With just the right balance of spices, these cookies deliver a nice warm and cozy feeling. They are a lovely treat for the winter holidays, and they will brighten up your whole home with their festive smell.

Skipping the egg in classic cookie recipes and making them plant-based was a challenging task, but I'm thrilled to pass them on to you. The trick is in the flour, sugar and butter ratio, so the only advice I would give you is to follow the recipe precisely. What excites me most about these cookies is their perfect texture: crisp on the outside and soft and chewy inside, exactly like a cookie should be. You can beautifully wrap them up and give them as presents to loved ones. They're also incredibly easy to make and quick to bake!

Makes: 18 cookies | Soy-free

⅔ cup (140 g) vegan butter, room temperature

¼ cup + 2 tbsp (90 g) muscovado sugar (see Notes)

6 tbsp (50 g) confectioners' sugar

2 tsp (10 ml) vanilla extract

1 cup (120 g) all-purpose flour

⅔ cup (70 g) ground almonds

½ tsp baking powder

½ tsp baking soda

¼ tsp sea salt

1½ tsp (4 g) ground cinnamon, divided

½ tsp ground ginger

¼ tsp ground nutmeg

¼ tsp freshly ground black pepper

1 tbsp granulated sugar

notes

Muscovado sugar can be easily purchased online, or you can substitute dark brown sugar.

Feel free to add chopped pecans or almonds to the batter. Nuts make a great pairing for these cookies.

In a saucepan, combine the vegan butter with the muscovado sugar and confectioners' sugar. Cook on medium-low heat, stirring constantly, for about 5 minutes, until the sugar is dissolved. Remove the pan from the heat and mix in the vanilla extract. Set aside to cool for 5 minutes.

In a bowl, mix the flour, ground almonds, baking powder, baking soda, salt, ½ teaspoon of the cinnamon, the ginger, nutmeg and black pepper. When the butter mixture is slightly cooled, pour it over the flour mixture. Using a wooden spoon, mix until well combined. Place the bowl in the fridge to cool for 15 to 20 minutes.

Preheat the oven to 375°F (180°C), and line two baking trays with parchment paper or silicone mats. Position the racks to divide the oven into thirds.

In a small bowl, mix the granulated sugar and remaining 1 teaspoon of cinnamon for the topping. Set aside.

Scoop out 1½ tablespoons of cookie dough and form into a ball. Each ball should measure around 1 ounce (25 to 27 g), which will make 18 equal-sized balls. Roll each ball in the sugar and cinnamon mix. Place the balls on the prepared baking sheet, about 2 inches (5 cm) apart (they will spread).

Bake for 10 to 12 minutes, until set and golden on the edges and soft on the inside. Keep an eye while they are baking and take them out of the oven when the edges are slightly set and start to brown—they cook very quickly and, for the right texture, it is better if they are slightly undercooked then overcooked. It is normal for the middle to still be soft to the touch after 10 to 12 minutes of baking; the cookies will completely set while cooling.

Let the cookies cool on the baking sheet for 1 minute, then transfer them to a wire rack to cool completely.

The cookies will keep well for up to 4 days at room temperature, stored in an airtight container.

spiced vegan honey & semolina cake

The combination of floral vegan honey, subtle cinnamon and cloves, vanilla custard and apricot jam is a nostalgic one for me. This cake is inspired by our Romanian traditional *albiniţa*, a honey layered cake that was always present on holiday menus. I am so fond of it that I even had to have this cake on my wedding menu. Using very basic and inexpensive ingredients, this cake delivers charming delicate flavors and entertains your taste buds, big time.

This is the type of cake that needs a few hours to set. Its moisture gets evenly distributed into the biscuit layers, making the final result soft and tender. With time, the flavors will also develop and spread throughout the cake.

Makes: 36 servings | Nut-free, soy-free

semolina custard

1¼ cups (300 ml) sweetened oat milk

½ cup (100 g) caster/superfine sugar

Zest from ½ lemon

Pinch of sea salt

⅓ cup (75 g) semolina flour

¼ cup (50 ml) vegan honey

2 tsp (10 ml) vanilla extract

¾ cup (180 g) vegan butter, room temperature

2 tbsp (30 ml) lemon juice

3 tbsp (45 ml) vegan cooking cream (see page 10)

vegan honey biscuit layers

2¼ cups (280 g) all-purpose flour, plus more for rolling

½ tsp baking soda

¼ tsp ground cinnamon

¼ tsp ground cloves

⅛ tsp sea salt

1½ tbsp (20 g) virgin coconut oil

2 tbsp (30 g) vegan butter

¼ cup (60 ml) sweetened oat milk

6 tbsp (50 g) confectioners' sugar

⅓ cup (75 ml) vegan honey (I used chamomile vegan honey)

1½ tsp (8 ml) vanilla extract

To make the Semolina Custard, add the oat milk, caster/superfine sugar, lemon zest and salt to a saucepan. Bring to a boil, then reduce to medium-low heat. Add the semolina flour and stir continuously. Simmer for 5 to 6 minutes, until thickened. Remove the pan from the heat and add the vegan honey and vanilla. Mix well to combine. Cover the surface of the custard with cling film and let it cool completely.

When the custard is at room temperature, place the vegan butter in the bowl of a stand mixer and whisk until creamy and slightly fluffy. Using a whisk, mix the cooled semolina custard to make it creamier again. With a spoon, add 2 to 3 tablespoons (30 to 45 ml) of Semolina Custard at a time into the creamed butter and whisk. Repeat until all the custard is added to the creamed butter. Then, add the lemon juice and cooking cream and give it a last stir; the mixture will be thick and smooth. Transfer to a bowl and refrigerate until ready to use.

Preheat the oven to 375°F (180°C), and line two baking sheets with parchment paper or silicone mats. Position the racks to divide the oven into thirds.

To make the biscuit layer, combine the flour, baking soda, cinnamon, cloves and salt in a bowl. Set aside.

To a saucepan, add the coconut oil, butter, oat milk and sugar. Cook on low until the sugar is dissolved and butter is melted, 3 to 5 minutes. Take the pan off the heat and let it cool completely. When cool, add the vegan honey and vanilla. Mix the liquids well.

Pour the vegan honey mixture into the flour and fold, using a spatula or a wooden spoon until just combined.

Transfer the dough to a floured work surface and knead to form a smooth, elastic dough. Divide the dough into four equal parts.

(continued)

spiced vegan honey & semolina cake (continued)

filling & topping

1 cup (240 g) apricot jam (see Notes)

1 tbsp (15 ml) lemon juice

1 tbsp (8 g) confectioners' sugar

notes

You can use any jam you like as filling: rosehip works beautifully here as well as raspberry or orange.

Keep in mind that this cake tends to get a bit too moist with time, so I wouldn't keep it for more than 3 days—not that I think it will last that long in any home without being eaten!

Take one of the sheets of parchment paper from the prepared tray and place it on your work surface. Take one piece of the dough and, using a rolling pin, dust the dough with some flour and roll the dough into a thin 9-inch (24-cm) square, directly on the parchment paper, which will make transferring the layer to the tray much easier, without breaking the biscuit.

Cut the edges, if necessary, so you get a clean square shape.

Transfer the biscuit layer to the tray and repeat the same process with the second piece of dough, trying to make all the layers as similar as possible.

Using a fork, poke holes in five to seven places in each biscuit layer. These holes will let the air circulate and it will ensure a flat biscuit without air bubbles.

Bake two layers at a time, for 5 to 6 minutes maximum in the preheated oven, until golden brown. Let the first two layers cool completely on a flat surface. The biscuit will harden and become crispy by the time it is cooled. Repeat the process with the rest of the dough.

Place the four layers on a clean, dry tray until assembling the cake. Be gentle as the layers can break easily. Keep at room temperature until ready to use.

To assemble the cake, place one biscuit layer on a plate or board. Add half of the Semolina Custard on top of the layer. Use an offset spatula to spread the filling evenly across the biscuit layer. Place another biscuit layer on top of the filling and gently press down with your hands, to ensure the layers stick together.

Mix the apricot jam with the lemon juice and spread the mixture evenly on top of the biscuit using a spoon. Top with another biscuit layer, then add the remaining Semolina Custard and spread evenly using an offset spatula. Add the last biscuit layer. Press gently to ensure all the layers stick together.

Cover the cake and refrigerate for 4 to 5 hours. This cake requires a bit of time so the biscuit layers can absorb some of the humidity of the filling and get soft and tender.

When ready to serve, place the cake on a cutting board. Trim the edges slightly if they are uneven. Using a chef's knife, cut six strips lengthwise, then slice each strip into approximately 1½-inch (4-cm) squares. To make this easier, cut the cake in half then cut each half into two equal strips. Repeat the process with the other half, then cut each strip into half, then each half into two. This way you will get equal slices without the fuss of measuring the cake.

Dust with the confectioners' sugar and place on a serving plate.

Place any leftovers in an airtight container and keep at room temperature for up to 3 days, covered with a towel.

carrot cake with homemade carrot jam

A flavor bomb bursting with spices, this carrot cake makes for a perfect special occasion cake. It has the great taste of a classic British carrot cake, nutty and earthy, but this version also comes with a joyful addition of carrot jam—which, in my opinion, should be made mandatory. This cake is rich, fragrant delightful, and everyone will love it. Also, the jam is so good you must have it in your breakfast routine (like I do), so maybe you'd like to double up on the amount you make. Trust me on this one!

Makes: 8 servings | Soy-free

carrot jam

5 oz (150 g) raw carrot

¾ cup + 2 tbsp (175 g) cane sugar, divided

1¼ cups (300 ml) filtered water

1 tbsp (15 ml) lemon juice

4 cardamom pods, crushed

1 small cinnamon stick

3 clove pods

2 dried juniper berry pods

carrot cake

1 cup (110 g) all-purpose flour

⅓ cup (40 g) whole wheat flour

2 tsp (10 g) baking powder

⅛ tsp baking soda

1 tsp ground Ceylon cinnamon

¼ tsp ground nutmeg

½ tsp ground ginger

½ tsp ground cardamom

1 tbsp (10 g) finely chopped walnuts

1 tbsp (10 g) finely chopped almonds

¼ cup (30 g) golden raisins

¼ tsp sea salt

½ cup (100 g) light brown sugar

3 tbsp (40 g) coconut sugar

⅓ cup (80 ml) vegetable oil

2 tsp (10 ml) apple cider vinegar

2 tsp (10 ml) unsweetened almond milk

2 tsp (10 ml) vanilla extract

¼ tsp orange zest

2 tsp (10 ml) good quality rum

6.5 oz (185 g) carrot, peeled and grated

To make the Carrot Jam, peel and grate the carrots, then place them in a bowl with about half of the sugar. Using a fork, give it a good stir. Let the carrots rest for about 1 hour.

Bring the water to a boil over medium heat. Add the carrot mixture and boil for 5 minutes on medium heat. Add the rest of the sugar, the lemon juice, cardamom pods, cinnamon stick, cloves and juniper berries. Lower the heat to medium–low and simmer the mixture for 40 to 50 minutes, until the carrots are soft and almost mushy, stirring occasionally. Transfer the hot jam to a clean, sterilized jar. Leave it to sit for 5 minutes without the lid on, then close the jar and turn it upside down, so that the fruit doesn't settle on the bottom of the jar. Leave it at room temperature to slowly cool down, then refrigerate for up to several weeks.

Preheat the oven to 370°F (175°C), set an oven rack in the middle position and line a 7-inch (18-cm) round cake pan with parchment paper. Set aside.

To make the Carrot Cake, stir the flours, baking powder, baking soda, cinnamon, nutmeg, ginger, cardamom, chopped nuts, raisins and salt in a bowl. Set aside.

In a separate bowl, whisk the brown sugar and coconut sugar with the oil, apple cider vinegar, almond milk, vanilla, orange zest and rum until the sugar is almost dissolved. Add the grated carrots to the wet mixture and stir until well combined.

Pour the carrot mixture over the dry ingredients. Using a spatula, fold the ingredients until combined, but don't overmix.

Pour the batter into the prepared cake pan. Bake the cake for 30 to 35 minutes. Test the center with a toothpick: if it comes out clean, the cake is done. If not, continue to bake until cooked through. Allow the cake to cool completely in the pan for 10 minutes then transfer to a wire rack. Cool the cake completely before frosting.

(continued)

carrot cake with homemade carrot jam (continued)

vegan cream cheese frosting

5 tbsp (75 g) vegan butter, room temperature

5 oz (150 g) vegan cream cheese, lightly salted, room temperature (such as plain Violife cream cheese)

1 tsp vanilla extract

Small pinch sea salt

½ cup (60 g) confectioners' sugar

for serving

2 tbsp (15 g) chopped toasted walnuts

To make the Vegan Cream Cheese Frosting, add the vegan butter, vegan cream cheese, vanilla and salt to the bowl of a stand mixer. Beat until lump-free, about 2 minutes. With the mixer on low, gradually add the confectioners' sugar and continue mixing until completely combined. Beat until creamy and fluffy and all the sugar has dissolved, 6 to 7 minutes. Refrigerate until ready to assemble the cake.

To split the cake in half horizontally, mark middle points around the side of the cake with toothpicks. Using toothpicks as a guide, cut through the cake with a long, sharp knife, using a back-and-forth motion.

Place the bottom layer of the cake on a serving plate with the cut side up. Spread 2 to 3 tablespoons (30 to 45 ml) of the Carrot Jam on the first layer. Using about half of the Vegan Cream Cheese Frosting, and an offset spatula, spread the frosting evenly across the bottom layer. Add the second layer of the cake and press gently with your hand. Top the cake with the rest of the frosting and spread evenly with an offset spatula.

Drizzle tablespoons (30 to 45 ml) of the Carrot Jam, all over the frosting. Sprinkle it with the toasted walnuts and refrigerate for at least 2 hours before serving.

The cake will keep well for up to 4 days, covered and refrigerated.

notes

The jam will keep for up to 3 months in the fridge. For longer storage, process the sealed jar for 5 minutes in a hot-water bath, then store.

If you'd like to make a larger quantity of this jam, I suggest using a reusable cloth tea bag or a ball tea strainer for the spices. This technique will help keep the whole spices in place, while infusing the jam with all the flavors.

star anise & pecan biscotti

The word biscotti derives from the Latin word *biscotus*, meaning "twice cooked" and while it might sound like a fuss, these are actually silly easy. The baking method was developed as a means of preservation, so these dry biscuits do keep well for a long time.

Dipping biscotti in hot, black and bitter coffee is the best reason to make this recipe. I live for this ritual, so there is no room here for a basic biscotti, only for the perfect one. That implies a very good crumb: when dipped into the hot liquid, it doesn't get soggy, but rather it takes just enough moisture to soften the crumb, without putting the cookie at high risk of breaking.

Ground star anise is the star here and does magic along with the pecans, so much so that—although you could make biscotti with almost any spice—I rarely use other flavors in my biscotti.

Makes: 24 biscotti | Soy-free

1 cup (130 g) all-purpose flour, plus more for rolling

½ cup + 1 tbsp (60 g) ground almonds

½ cup (110 g) light brown sugar

½ cup (50 g) pecans, chopped (see Note)

½ tsp ground star anise

2 tsp (9 g) baking powder

½ tsp baking soda

⅛ tsp sea salt

4 tsp (20 ml) maple syrup

1 tbsp (15 ml) unsweetened oat milk

2 tbsp (32 g) applesauce

Preheat the oven to 320°F (150°C), set an oven rack in the middle position and prepare a baking sheet with parchment paper or a silicone mat.

In a bowl, combine the all-purpose flour, ground almonds, sugar, pecans, ground star anise, baking powder, baking soda and sea salt. Mix and set aside.

In a separate bowl, mix the maple syrup, oat milk and applesauce to combine. Pour the liquid mixture over the dry ingredients and, using a wooden spoon, mix until combined and the dough comes together. If the mixture is too dry, add an additional 2 to 3 teaspoons (10 to 15 ml) of oat milk, but no more than that.

Transfer the dough to a floured work surface. Divide the dough in half and shape each piece into a 9½-inch (24-cm) log. Place the logs on the prepared baking sheet and bake for 15 minutes. Reduce the heat to 305°F (140°C) and continue baking for another 15 minutes, until slightly brown on the surface. Allow the logs to cool for 10 minutes. Increase the oven temperature to 320°F (150°C).

With a serrated knife, gently cut the logs slightly diagonally, into 12 slices per log. Place the biscotti on the baking sheet again, cut side down. Bake at 320°F (150°C) until lightly browned, about 10 minutes, turning once. Transfer the cookies to a wire rack to cool.

These biscuits have a long shelf life. Keep them in an airtight container for up to 3 weeks or even more.

note

You can substitute the pecans with walnuts, almonds or macadamia nuts.

saffron panna cotta with rose & raspberry coulis

This Italian panna cotta borrows a couple of Middle Eastern flavors and is one of my favorites when it comes to cold desserts. The rich, flavorful saffron gives warmth and a stunning color to the dessert, while the Rose & Raspberry Coulis complements the taste of the vegan custard with its floral and bright flavor. Coulis is a classic French sauce and is basically a thin sauce made from pureed and strained fruits or vegetables. This is an elegant, silky-smooth dessert and something to look forward to at the end of a meal.

Makes: 4 servings | Gluten-free, nut-free, soy-free, refined sugar-free

panna cotta

1¼ cups (300 ml) unsweetened oat milk

¾ cup + 2 tsp (200 ml) vegan cooking cream (see page 10)

½ tsp agar agar powder

2 tbsp (30 ml) agave nectar

⅛ tsp sea salt

10–15 saffron threads

1½ cinnamon sticks

rose & raspberry coulis

1 cup (120 g) fresh raspberries

2 tsp (10 ml) lemon juice

3 tbsp (50 ml) agave nectar

2 tbsp (30 ml) rosewater

1 tsp vanilla extract

Grease six serving cups or ramekins with a light coating of sunflower oil or any neutral oil. Set aside.

To make the Panna Cotta, place the oat milk, cooking cream, agar agar powder, agave nectar and sea salt in a saucepan. Whisk and bring to a boil over medium heat, then reduce heat to low. Add the saffron threads and the cinnamon sticks and simmer for 4 to 5 minutes, stirring continuously.

Remove the cinnamon sticks and carefully pour the hot mixture into the serving cups, using a sieve to strain the saffron threads. Refrigerate for at least 1½ hours, or until the Panna Cotta is well set.

Meanwhile, prepare the Rose & Raspberry Coulis. Place the raspberries in a bowl and smash them well using a fork. Add the lemon juice, agave nectar, rosewater and vanilla. Mix well to combine. Use a fine strainer to strain the puree into a clean bowl. Set aside.

To serve, turn each ramekin upside-down onto a serving plate. If the Panna Cotta doesn't drop out, carefully dip the bottom of the ramekin in a bowl of warm water to loosen it. Serve with a good drizzle of the Rose & Raspberry Coulis.

The Panna Cotta and Rose & Raspberry Coulis will keep well for up to 3 days, refrigerated and covered.

wild berries & cinnamon streusel muffins

Everyone who knows me understands my need for a bite of sweetness at the end of every meal, including breakfast, and these muffins are in my top three favorites. I find the marriage of whole wheat flavor and the tangy wild berries to be just perfect for my morning cravings. But feel free to use any fruit you'd like; sliced apples, pears or apricots are divine here!

These muffins are gently sweetened and have an earthy aroma and a light, fluffy crumb. The cinnamon streusel enhances the sweetness just a bit, while adding a crunchy dimension that makes the muffins perfect. If I make these a day before, I'm a happy human ready to get on with a new day.

Makes: 12 muffins | Nut-free, soy-free

cinnamon streusel

¾ cup (90 g) all-purpose flour (see Note)

⅓ cup + 1 tbsp (80 g) cane sugar

1 tsp ground cinnamon

Pinch of sea salt

¼ cup (60 g) vegan butter, melted

muffins

1½ cups (200 g) all-purpose flour (see Note)

1 cup (130 g) whole wheat flour

½ cup (90 g) coconut sugar

2 tbsp (20 g) cane sugar

½ tsp ground cinnamon

2 tsp (9 g) baking powder

¼ tsp baking soda

½ tsp sea salt

Zest from 1 lemon

6 tbsp (90 ml) olive oil

¼ cup (50 ml) plain coconut yogurt

1⅓ cups (320 ml) unsweetened oat milk

2 tsp (10 ml) lemon juice

2 tsp (10 ml) vanilla extract

7 oz (200 g) wild berries, fresh or frozen

To make the Cinnamon Streusel, combine the flour, sugar, cinnamon and salt in a small bowl. Using a fork, give it a good mix. Pour the melted butter over the mixture and mix again until well combined. Set aside.

Preheat the oven to 370°F (175°C), set an oven rack in the middle position and line a muffin tray with paper muffin cups. Set aside.

To make the muffins, add the flours, sugars, cinnamon, baking powder, baking soda, salt and lemon zest to a medium bowl and mix well with a wooden spoon. Set aside.

In a separate bowl, mix the olive oil, coconut yogurt, oat milk, lemon juice and vanilla extract. Pour the liquid mixture over the dry ingredients and gently mix until everything is just incorporated. Add the wild berries and fold into the batter with circular movements, without overmixing.

Fill the muffin cups two-thirds full and bake for about 25 minutes, until risen, firm to the touch and a skewer inserted in the middle comes out clean.

Leave the muffins in the tin to cool for 5 minutes, then transfer to a wire rack to cool completely.

Keep in an airtight container at room temperature for up to 4 days.

note

You can make this recipe even higher in fiber by replacing the all-purpose flour with an equal amount of whole wheat flour.

matcha rice pudding with blueberry compote

The grains of rice in this pudding graciously carry the flavors and soothing properties of matcha, vanilla and citrus, resulting in a rich, silky pudding that feels like self-care. For this recipe, I like to use Arborio rice or any round grain rice that I would use for risotto. Be patient while cooking this, as rice puddings are notorious for sticking to the pan. At the end, fold in a good quality matcha powder and top with the colorful blueberry compote to give the pudding a light and fresh acidity as well as more depth of flavor.

Makes: 2 servings | Gluten-free, nut-free, soy-free, refined sugar-free

blueberry compote
¾ cup (120 g) fresh blueberries (see Note)

4 tsp (20 ml) agave nectar

1 tbsp (15 ml) lemon juice

⅛ tsp ground cinnamon

rice pudding
⅔ cup (100 g) Arborio rice

2¼ cups (550 ml) sweetened oat milk, plus more if needed

2 tbsp + 2 tsp (40 ml) agave nectar

¼ tsp sea salt

¼ tsp lemon zest

¼ tsp orange zest

⅓ cup + 1½ tbsp (100 ml) vegan cooking cream (see page 10), divided

½ tsp high-quality matcha powder, plus more for garnish

2 tsp (10 ml) vanilla extract

Toasted pine nuts, for garnish, optional

To make the Blueberry Compote, add the blueberries, agave and lemon juice to a saucepan. Stir well to combine, then bring it to a boil over medium heat. Gently smash some of the blueberries using a fork to release some of their juices. Cook for 1 to 3 minutes on high heat, until a dark rich color is achieved. Add the cinnamon and mix to combine. Remove from the heat and set aside.

To make the Rice Pudding, place the rice in a heavy saucepan and add the oat milk, agave nectar and sea salt. Cook gently over low heat for 40 to 50 minutes, stirring regularly. If it starts to dry out before the rice is cooked, add more oat milk (approximately ¼ cup [60 ml]), and continue to stir. When the rice is almost cooked, add the lemon zest and orange zest. Stir to combine and cook for another 2 minutes.

Meanwhile, combine ⅓ cup (80 ml) of the cooking cream with the matcha powder in a small cup and stir until completely dissolved.

When the rice is completely cooked, remove the Rice Pudding from the heat and add the matcha cream mixture and vanilla extract. Stir to combine.

Plate the Rice Pudding in bowls and top it with cooled Blueberry Compote and a drizzle of the remaining 1½ tbsp (20 ml) of cooking cream. Dust with a bit of matcha powder and sprinkle with toasted pine nuts if desired. Serve and enjoy.

Both the Rice Pudding and Blueberry Compote are best served the same day, but they will keep well for up to 2 days, refrigerated, in airtight containers. Reheat the pudding before serving.

note

You can use other fruits for the compote: strawberries or rhubarb would go wonderfully in this recipe.

gluten-free pumpkin & white chocolate oat bars

Using wholesome ingredients for a delicious outcome, these oat bars have an excellent reputation for a good reason. It's a delicious and nutritious snack, and I love to complete my savory breakfast with an oat bar like this, especially when smooth, flavorful pumpkin puree is involved.

These also have a few delicious vegan white chocolate chunks in them and are friendly to those who avoid gluten. For nice chocolate curls, I like to use a vegetable peeler to shred the chocolate. Handle the chocolate with aluminum foil, so it does not melt on your fingers.

The bars are lightly sweetened (you can top them with extra maple syrup, as I did) and have a chewy texture and a nice spice kick for a truly mouthwatering dessert snack!

Makes: 9 servings | Gluten-free, soy-free, refined sugar-free

pumpkin frosting

7 oz (200 g) pumpkin puree
1½ tbsp (25 ml) maple syrup
2 tsp (10 ml) vanilla extract
3 tbsp (30 g) coconut sugar
⅓ cup (80 ml) sweetened oat milk
⅓ cup (80 g) almond butter
½ tsp ground cinnamon
¼ tsp ground cloves
¼ tsp ground ginger

oat bars

1 tbsp (7 g) ground flaxseeds
2 tbsp (30 ml) water
1¼ cups (120 g) oat flour
⅔ cup (50 g) quick-cooking oats
2 tsp (10 g) baking powder
½ tsp sea salt
3 oz (80 g) vegan white chocolate, chopped (see Note)
⅓ cup + 1 tbsp (100 ml) unsweetened oat milk
2 tbsp (30 ml) maple syrup

for serving

2–3 tbsp (30–45 ml) maple syrup
1 oz (20 g) vegan white chocolate (see Note)

To make the frosting, place the pumpkin puree, maple syrup, vanilla, coconut sugar, oat milk, almond butter, cinnamon, cloves and ginger in a high-speed blender. Blend well until smooth and creamy and the coconut sugar is dissolved. Reserve ½ cup (135 g) of the frosting to use in the oatcake, and refrigerate the remaining mixture.

Preheat the oven to 370°F (175°C) and line an 8-inch (20-cm) square cake pan with parchment paper.

In a small cup, mix the flaxseeds and water. Set aside for 5 minutes to thicken.

Add the flour, oats, baking powder, salt and chopped chocolate to a bowl. Mix to combine. Pour the flaxseed mixture over the dry ingredients, together with the oat milk, maple syrup and the reserved ½ cup (135 g) of the pumpkin frosting. Use a wooden spoon to mix until well combined.

Transfer the batter to the prepared cake pan. Level the batter using the back of a spoon and bake for 25 to 30 minutes, or until a toothpick inserted in the center comes out clean. Let cool for 5 minutes in the pan, then transfer to a cooling rack and let cool completely.

Place the cake on a serving board and spread the pumpkin frosting evenly, using the back of a clean spoon or an offset spatula. Drizzle with the maple syrup and shred the vegan white chocolate on top. Cut into nine squares and serve.

The bars keep, refrigerated, in an airtight container for up to 3 days.

note

If you cannot find a vegan white chocolate, this cake also pairs well with a dark or vegan milk chocolate.

coffee, nuts & seeds

Filled with nutty, earthy and rich flavors, this chapter is a true joy. It mixes a variety of classic and modern techniques and my approach is to create astounding sweets that just happen to be vegan.

Aside from delighting yourself with delicious creations, this chapter will also show you some tips and tricks in vegan baking. Learn how to master leavened vegan doughs and create spectacular fluffy desserts, how to bake with no gluten and what binder to use instead of eggs. In my Pecan & Plum Crescents (page 126) you will discover an easy trick for creating super flaky and tender cookies just by adding a splash of alcohol into the dough.

Ready to bake? Try my Six-Layer Mocha Cake (page 116)! This rich and robust cake, with six layers of buttercream, is the triumph of marrying chocolate with coffee. The Heavenly Poppy Seed & Raisin Babka (page 119) will become your best friend during the winter holidays and to get ahead of the average cookie recipe, try the Black Sesame Seed & Matcha Cookies (page 122). They are super quick and easy to bake, with notable flavors of matcha and black sesame seed butter.

six-layer mocha cake

Inspired by the Hungarian Dobos torte, here is a plant-based chocolate and coffee cake that you'll fall in love with. A Dobos torte is a simple yet elegant cake, layered with irresistible chocolate buttercream and topped with caramelized sugar glass. It was very popular, especially in the confectioneries of northwestern Romania, during the communist and post-communist period. This was also my sister's preferred birthday cake, and my mom used to add a bit of coffee to the buttercream (and she still does). That's how I got the idea—only I use five times more coffee in the buttercream and layers too, due to my intense love of coffee.

This cake is a true gem, and you will definitely ask for a second helping. It's buttery, not overly sweet and full of coffee and chocolate flavors. It also has a chewy bite and a generous dark chocolate sticky ganache on top, and both features are to die for.

Makes: 8–10 servings | Nut-free, soy-free

biscuit layers

⅓ cup (75 g) caster/superfine sugar

3 tbsp (45 ml) espresso shot, room temperature

⅓ cup (80 ml) hot water

2 tsp (10 ml) vanilla extract

⅛ tsp baking soda

1½ tsp (7 g) baking powder

1 tbsp (15 ml) lemon juice

6 tbsp (90 ml) sunflower oil

3 cups (360 g) all-purpose flour, plus more for rolling

½ tsp sea salt

To make the Biscuit Layers, add the sugar to a saucepan and let it caramelize on low heat, without stirring, for about 5 minutes.

While the sugar is caramelizing, mix the espresso shot and hot water in a small cup.

When the sugar melts and turns a light brown color, add the coffee mixture and vanilla and increase the heat to medium. Cook for a few seconds over medium heat then set aside to cool.

In a separate cup, mix the baking soda and baking powder, then pour in the lemon juice. Stir and let the ingredients react (it will get very bubbly) then pour into the coffee and sugar mixture, along with the oil. This step will ensure that the layers will not rise too much, but will create a crisp, tender texture.

In a medium bowl, mix the flour and salt. Add 2 to 3 tablespoons (16 to 24 g) of the flour mixture at a time to the saucepan with the coffee mixture. Stir gently with a spatula then repeat until all of the flour mixture is added. When it feels hard to mix with the spatula, use your hands and knead the dough until all ingredients are well combined. It should result in a flexible, elastic dough. Transfer the dough to a floured work surface and shape it into a ball. Cover and let sit for 15 minutes.

Meanwhile, preheat the oven to 360°F (170°C), and line two baking sheets with parchment paper or silicone mats. Position the racks to divide the oven into thirds.

Divide the dough into six equal pieces, approximately 3 ounces (90 g) each. Flour your hands and a rolling pin and roll out each piece of dough into an 8½-inch (22-cm) disk. Use a pan lid of the same dimension to guide you with the shape. Don't stress too much about making perfect circles, you can trim the edges at the end.

Place two layers on each baking sheet and bake for no more than 7 to 8 minutes. The layers are thin and cook quickly, so keep an eye on the oven. When the disks are slightly brown on the edges, take them out and repeat the process with the last two layers. If your oven is small, cook only two layers at a time.

(continued)

six-layer mocha cake (continued)

mocha buttercream

1 cup + 2 tsp (250 ml) vegan cooking cream (see page 10)

⅓ cup + 1 tbsp (100 ml) sweetened oat milk

½ cup + 2 tbsp (130 g) light brown sugar

⅛ tsp sea salt

5 oz (150 g) vegan dark chocolate, 65% cacao

2 tbsp (15 g) cornstarch

¼ cup + 2 tsp (70 ml) espresso shot, room temperature

2 tsp (10 ml) vanilla extract

7 tbsp (100 g) vegetable butter, cubed and at room temperature

chocolate ganache

⅓ cup (80 ml) vegan cooking cream (see page 10)

5 oz (150 g) vegan dark chocolate, 65% cacao, chopped

If you want to amp up the coffee flavor of the frosting, combine 1 to 2 teaspoons (2 to 4 g) of espresso powder with 2 teaspoons (10 ml) of oat milk. Pour the mixture into the frosting and whisk to combine.

Let the Biscuit Layers cool completely on wire racks.

Meanwhile, prepare the Mocha Buttercream. In a saucepan, bring the cooking cream, oat milk, sugar and salt to a boil together over medium heat. Turn the heat to low and add the chopped chocolate. Stir gently until all the chocolate is dissolved.

In a small cup, mix the cornstarch and espresso shot and stir well until dissolved. Pour into the chocolate mix and simmer on low for 5 minutes. Remove the pan from the heat, add the vanilla and mix. Set the pan aside to cool, covered with cling film directly on the surface of the custard, to prevent it from forming a thick skin.

Place the butter into the bowl of a stand mixer and whisk thoroughly to remove any lumps. Cream the butter for 5 to 7 minutes, or until it starts to get fluffy, then add 2 tablespoons (30 ml) at a time of the cooled chocolate custard. Make sure the chocolate custard is room temperature.

Repeat the process until all the custard is incorporated. It should result in a creamy, light-colored frosting. Taste test the frosting when creaming the butter and custard. If you'd like an even stronger coffee flavor see the directions in the Note.

To assemble the cake, place a small dollop of buttercream in the middle of a serving plate. Place one Biscuit Layer on top. The buttercream will ensure the cake won't slide off the plate. Divide the remaining buttercream into six equal portions and spread one portion of the buttercream on top of the first layer. Top with the second Biscuit Layer and gently press down with your palm. Repeat the process and frost the top of the last layer. Refrigerate for at least 30 minutes so the buttercream starts to harden.

To make the Chocolate Ganache, place the cooking cream in a saucepan and cook on medium until hot, but not boiling, about 3 minutes. Add the chopped chocolate and stir gently until melted. Let the mixture cool for at least 10 minutes before decorating the cake.

When the cake is chilled, spread the ganache on the top and sides of the cake to seal in crumbs. Level with a spatula, and then refrigerate for at least 6 hours, or overnight. This cake requires a bit of chilling time so the Biscuit Layers can absorb some of the humidity of the buttercream and get soft and tender.

This cake will keep for up to 6 days, covered and refrigerated. This is the type of cake that gets even better after the first 2 days. Its moisture becomes more evenly distributed and the flavors combine and spread throughout the cake.

heavenly poppy seed & raisin babka

Made of a fine leavened brioche dough and filled with a milky, poppy seed cream, this babka is right on the edge between a cake and a sweet bread. It also holds a special place in my heart, as I grew up with this, but under the name of *cozonac*. It is one of the most symbolic foods of any major event or celebration in my home country: Christmas, Easter, weddings and funerals.

Pour yourself a glass of wine and take your time when making this; this brioche technique needs some additional time for fermentation and proofing, but it will ensure you a fluffy and stretchy texture. The reward of eating it is definitely worth the effort and you may keep this recipe close, as the dough is the best canvas for many other beautifully leavened desserts.

Makes: 10–12 servings | Nut-free, soy-free

brioche dough

- 1 tbsp (10 g) fresh yeast or 1¼ tsp (5 g) dry or instant dry yeast (see Notes)
- ¼ cup + 2½ tbsp (100 ml) unsweetened oat milk, lukewarm, divided
- 2 cups (250 g) all-purpose flour, divided
- 3 tbsp (40 g) caster/superfine sugar
- 1 tbsp (10 g) light brown sugar
- ¼ tsp baking soda
- 2 tsp (10 ml) vanilla extract
- Zest from ½ orange
- Zest from ½ lemon
- ¼ tsp sea salt
- ¼ cup (60 ml) sparkling water, room temperature
- 2½ tbsp (35 g) vegan butter, cubed and at room temperature

To make the dough, crumble the fresh yeast into a small bowl, then add 2½ tablespoons (40 ml) of the lukewarm oat milk and stir with a wooden spoon to dissolve. Add 3 tablespoons (24 g) of the flour and mix again until a soft batter forms. Set aside at room temperature for 10 to 15 minutes, or until doubled in size.

In a separate bowl, mix the remaining ¼ cup (60 ml) of oat milk, the sugars, baking soda, vanilla, citrus zests and salt. Add the sparkling water to this mixture, then immediately move to the next step. The sparkling water should be added to the flour as soon as possible.

In a stand mixer fitted with the dough hook, place the remaining 1¾ cups (226 g) of flour. Add the milk and sparkling water mixture along with the risen yeast. Mix at low speed until a dough forms, then mix an additional 5 minutes on medium speed. Add about a quarter of the butter at a time, and mix on low for 20 minutes in total.

The next step is optional, but to develop the structure of the gluten even more, I like to do an extra knead of the dough on a lightly floured surface and slap and fold a few times (10 to 15 times are enough for this step). This is a technique I learned from the French baker Richard Bertinet.

Finally, form the dough into a ball, place it into a large, oiled bowl and let the dough rise at room temperature for 1 hour and 30 minutes, or until doubled in volume (see Notes).

(continued)

heavenly poppy seed & raisin babka (continued)

poppy seed filling

1 cup (150 g) poppy seeds

⅓ cup (75 ml) unsweetened oat milk

2 tbsp (25 ml) vegan cooking cream (see page 10)

⅓ cup (80 g) light brown sugar

Zest from ½ lemon

Pinch of sea salt

1 tsp vanilla extract

¼ cup (40 g) raisins

¼ cup (60 ml) fresh orange juice

2 tsp (10 ml) rum

for serving

1 tbsp (15 ml) unsweetened oat milk

2 tsp (10 ml) vegan honey or agave nectar

notes

For sweet brioches like this, I like to use fresh yeast because it stays active longer and I find it more stable during proofing. However, this recipe works just fine using dry yeast.

Keep in mind that this sweet bread tends to get dry with time, so my favorite way of storing it is wrapping it up in cling film and placing it in a dry and cool place, or at room temperature. It will keep for 4 to 5 days.

Meanwhile, prepare the filling. Place the poppy seeds in a blender jar and pulse a few times, until the seeds are almost all broken. Transfer to a clean bowl.

In a saucepan, add the milk, cooking cream, sugar, lemon zest and salt and bring to a boil. When it hits the boiling point, pour the boiling mixture over the poppy seeds. Mix with a wooden spatula. Add the vanilla and let the seeds absorb the milk and cool completely.

In a separate bowl, place the raisins, orange juice and rum. Set them aside to hydrate in the juice for at least 1 hour or more.

When the dough is doubled in size, lightly flour your working surface. Divide the dough in half, shape each half into a ball and cover with a towel.

Line a 9½ x 4–inch (24 x 11–cm) loaf pan with baking paper.

Take one ball and roll it into a 12 x 14–inch (30 x 35–cm) rectangle. Scoop out half of the poppy seed filling and place on top one piece of the rolled dough. Using an offset spatula, spread the filling evenly around the dough.

Strain the raisins and sprinkle half of them over the poppy seed mixture. Use both hands to roll up the rectangle like a roulade, starting from the long side closest to you and ending at the other long end. Press it to seal the dampened end onto the roulade, then use both hands to even out the roll into a perfect, thick roll and let it rest on its seam. Repeat the process with the second piece of dough and remaining filling.

Take the two rolls of dough and twist them together all the way down the length of the roll. Carefully place the twist in the prepared loaf tin, tucking the ends under slightly, if needed. Cover with a clean and loose plastic bag and leave to rise at room temperature, until it has almost doubled in size, roughly 1 hour 15 minutes (see Notes). Make sure the brioche has enough room to rise under the cover. Meanwhile, preheat the oven to 370°F (175°C).

Gently brush the top of the proofed loaf with the oat milk and bake the loaf in the lower level of the preheated oven for 50 to 60 minutes, until it is reddish brown on top and cooked through. Take it out and immediately brush the top with the vegan honey or agave. This step will give the loaf a beautiful shiny crust. Allow the loaf to cool slightly before removing it from the pan to cool completely.

notes

If you're not sure if your room is warm enough and suited for a proper proofing, use this tip to ensure development of the yeast: turn on the light of your oven and keep the heat and ventilation off. Place your covered dough into the oven. The closed oven together with the light will generate the perfect warm and humid environment so that the dough can proof and rise to full potential.

black sesame seed & matcha cookies

This recipe is guaranteed not to disappoint any cookie connoisseur! These are crackly on the outside, moist and chewy when you bite into them, and all the best parts of a classic cookie are fired up by the nutty flavor of black sesame butter, as well as the gentle taste of matcha. These precious cookies are perfect to dip into a warm glass of oat milk. Did I mention how easy it is to make these? They only require 10 to 12 minutes of baking time, and you just need to mix the flour with the melted butter and sugars, chill the dough for a bit, shape it into small balls and then put these straight into the oven.

Makes: 18 cookies | Soy-free

⅔ cup (140 g) vegan butter, cubed

1 cup + 2 tbsp (140 g) confectioners' sugar

2 tsp (10 ml) vanilla extract

Zest from ½ lemon

1 cup (120 g) all-purpose flour

⅔ cup (70 g) ground almonds

½ tsp baking powder

¼ tsp baking soda

⅛ tsp sea salt

2 tsp (4 g) matcha powder (see Notes)

1 tbsp (16 g) black sesame seed butter (see Notes)

In a saucepan, cook the butter and sugar on low for about 5 minutes, until the butter is melted and the sugar has completely dissolved, stirring continuously. Add the vanilla and lemon zest and set aside to cool slightly.

In a separate bowl, mix the flour, ground almonds, baking powder, baking soda and salt until well combined. Pour the butter and sugar mixture into the flour mix and stir with a wooden spoon.

Measure the dough and divide it in half. Place each half in a separate bowl and add the matcha powder to one and the black sesame butter to the other. Mix gently, until well combined. Refrigerate both bowls for at least 20 minutes.

Preheat the oven to 375°F (180°C), and line two baking sheets with parchment paper or silicone mats. Position the racks to divide the oven into thirds.

Take the dough out of the fridge. Scoop out about 2 teaspoons (10 g) of dough from each bowl, combine them gently in your hands and roll into a ball. Do not over-roll, roll just enough to form a ball. Each ball should be approximately 1 ounce (25 to 27 g). Place the balls on the prepared baking sheet, about 2 inches (5 cm) apart (they will spread).

Bake for 10 to 12 minutes, until flattened and set on the edges. They should remain slightly soft in the center. Let the cookies cool on the baking sheet for 5 minutes, then transfer them to a wire rack to cool completely.

These cookies will keep well for up to 3 to 4 days, in an airtight container, at room temperature. You can also freeze them for up to 2 months.

notes

You can use any type of matcha powder (culinary grade is okay), but I personally like to use a ceremonial grade matcha because the flavor is stronger and better refined.

Black sesame butter should be easy to find at any local health shop. But, you can also make it at home. Simply toast 1 cup (112 g) of whole black sesame seeds in the oven at 370°F (175°C) for 5 to 7 minutes, then blend them in a high-speed blender with 2 teaspoons (10 ml) of neutral oil until you get a smooth seed butter, similar to peanut butter. Alternatively, simply use tahini paste, which is the seed butter made from toasted white sesame seeds, instead of the black sesame seeds.

coffee parfait with boba pearls & biscotti

This fusion dessert might be my latest obsession: Taiwanese boba milk tea meets European biscotti and vegan custard! With a base of espresso-soaked biscotti, the parfait is built up by a fluffy layer of whipped cream, followed by the irresistible velvety white chocolate and coffee cream custard. All those layers are gloriously topped with the fun, soft and chewy boba pearls that hold a beautiful, caramelized taste due to the muscovado sugar syrup. Serve these as a fun treat at your next brunch.

Makes: 6 servings | Soy-free

coffee cream

10 oz (270 g) full-fat coconut milk, solids only

1½ tbsp (20 g) muscovado sugar (see Note)

⅛ tsp sea salt

3 tsp (8 g) cornstarch

2 tsp (10 ml) water

7 oz (200 g) vegan white chocolate, chopped

2 tsp (4 g) espresso powder

2 tsp (10 ml) vanilla extract

parfaits

½ batch of Star Anise & Pecan Biscotti (page 105)

⅓ cup (80 ml) espresso, chilled

4.5 oz (130 g) sweetened vegan whipped cream

boba pearls

6 oz (160 g) black tapioca pearls, medium size (WuFuYuan™ brand works best)

2 qts (1.8 L) water

¼ cup (50 g) muscovado sugar (see Note)

note

Muscovado sugar can be purchased online, or you can substitute dark brown sugar.

To make the Coffee Cream, place the coconut milk solids in a saucepan with the sugar and salt and bring to a boil on medium heat.

Meanwhile, in a small cup, mix the cornstarch and water until the cornstarch dissolves.

Turn the heat to low and pour in the cornstarch mixture, stirring constantly. Simmer until the mixture starts to thicken, about 3 minutes, then take the pan off the heat. Add the chopped white chocolate and stir to melt the chocolate.

When the chocolate is melted, add the espresso powder and vanilla and stir. Cover the saucepan with a lid and let cool completely.

To assemble the Parfaits, cut the biscotti in irregular pieces and add them to the bottom of each of six parfait glass, using approximately two biscotti per glass. Add 2 to 3 teaspoons (10 to 15 ml) of chilled espresso on top, to soak the biscotti. Add 2 to 3 tablespoons (30 to 45 ml) of whipped cream on top of the biscotti.

Divide the Coffee Cream into six equal portions and pour a portion into each glass. Refrigerate for at least 2 hours.

Make the Boba Pearls right before serving. Fill a bowl with ice water and set aside. Fill a large pot with water and bring to a boil. Reduce the heat to medium and add the boba pearls. When the boba pearls float to the top, reduce the heat to medium and cover the pot. Cook for 2 to 3 minutes maximum. Remove the boba pearls with a slotted spoon and place them directly into the bowl of ice water to let them cool for a few minutes.

To a small bowl, add 2 to 3 tablespoons (30 to 45 ml) of the boiling water, then mix in the muscovado sugar and set aside.

Drain the tapioca pearls and transfer them to the muscovado sugar syrup. Cover and set aside for 10 minutes to allow them to infuse. The Boba Pearls should be chewy and sweet. Keep the boba in the syrup until ready to assemble. You will also be using the syrup to top the parfait.

Top the chilled parfait with the Boba Pearls and drizzle 1 to 2 teaspoons (5 to 10 ml) of the sugar syrup in each glass. Enjoy right away!

These Parfaits are best consumed on the same day they are made. However, for a longer shelf life, simply build the Parfaits in glasses on the day of serving.

pecan & plum crescents

Similar to the Jewish rugelach cookies, these crescents are very popular in Romanian food culture. Traditionally, they were filled with our beloved *silvoiță*, which is a sugar-free homemade plum jam and a true delicacy. Because I know this jam is not easy to find, the closest thing is dried plums, as their taste is so similar to our *silvoiță*.

I am super happy to share these delicious cookies with you, as this veganized version of the pastry is super tender and melts in your mouth. It perfectly resembles the original version made with loads of butter and lard and that is thanks to the added white wine, which helps create a flaky dough. Unlike water, alcohol doesn't develop as much gluten in the pastry. Made with stevia as a sweetener, these cookies are almost refined sugar-free. They taste so rich and I would easily say they are addictive.

Makes: 25 crescents | Soy-free

filling

1¼ cups (200 g) dried plums, pitted

1 tbsp (15 ml) lemon juice

1 cup (100 g) finely chopped pecans

½ tsp ground cinnamon

dough

3 tbsp (45 ml) unsweetened oat milk, warm

½ tsp dry yeast

1¾ cups (230 g) all-purpose flour, plus more for kneading

3 tbsp (20 g) ground almonds

Zest from ½ lemon

¼ tsp sea salt

3½ tbsp (50 g) virgin coconut oil, slightly melted

¼ cup (50 g) vegan butter, room temperature, cubed

15 drops liquid stevia

2 tsp (10 ml) vanilla extract

2 tbsp (30 ml) white wine or bourbon whiskey

for serving

½ cup (60 g) confectioners' sugar, optional

To make the Filling, place the pitted dried plums and lemon juice in a high-speed blender and blend until a fine paste forms. Transfer the paste to a bowl and stir in the pecans and cinnamon. Set aside.

To prepare the Dough, place the warm oat milk in a cup. Add the dry yeast and set aside for 5 minutes, without stirring, until the yeast has completely dissolved.

In a medium bowl, place the all-purpose flour. Add the ground almonds, lemon zest and sea salt. Mix, then set aside. Add the coconut oil and vegan butter to the flour mixture. Mix, using a spatula or your hands, until the mixture resembles wet sand. Set aside.

Pour the oat and yeast mixture into the flour along with the liquid stevia, vanilla and alcohol. Mix with a wooden spoon or with your hand, until the dough comes together. Transfer the dough to a floured surface and knead lightly, until everything is well combined and the flour has absorbed all the liquid. Divide the dough in half and form each into a ball.

Preheat the oven to 370°F (175°C), set an oven rack in the middle position and line a baking sheet with parchment paper or a silicon mat.

Using a rolling pin, roll out one ball into a thin 10½-inch (27-cm) disk. Using a sharp knife, cut the dough into quarters, then each quarter into three triangles, to form twelve triangles.

At the base of each triangle (the wider end), add ½ to 1 teaspoon of the filling. Starting at the base, roll the dough up over the filling so that each cookie becomes a crescent. Arrange the roll-ups on the lined baking sheet, making sure the points are tucked under the cookies. Repeat this process with the rest of the dough.

Bake the cookies for 10 to 12 minutes, until they are puffed and slightly golden on the edges.

Remove the trays from the oven and immediately use a sifter to coat the cookies with confectioners' sugar (if using). Let the crescents cool on the trays, then transfer to a serving plate. Sift more confectioners' sugar on top of the cookies before serving.

Store in an airtight container up to 6 days.

coffee, cinnamon & walnut tea cake

I present to you your new favorite loaf cake! With a buttery and airy crumb, this cake has a generous layer of walnuts, coffee and chocolate in the middle. As with any of my cakes, you couldn't tell this has no eggs or dairy. Not long ago I brought this to my Italian friend, Georgia, and when she first bit into a slice of this cake, her eyes widened and she smiled gorgeously. Her reaction confirmed why I loved this cake so much and I have no doubt you will too!

Enjoy it with a mandatory coffee, tea or plant-based milk.

Makes: 10 servings | Soy-free

coffee swirl

2 tbsp (25 g) light brown sugar

2 tbsp (20 g) coconut sugar

1 tsp espresso powder

¼ tsp ground cinnamon

3 tbsp (15 g) ground walnuts

0.5 oz (10 g) vegan dark chocolate, 70% cacao, finely chopped

tea cake

⅓ cup (75 g) vegan butter, room temperature

⅔ cup (135 g) light brown sugar, powdered (see Notes)

2 tbsp (30 ml) sunflower oil

2 tsp (10 ml) vanilla extract

⅓ cup (75 g) sweetened oat milk

1 tbsp (15 ml) apple cider vinegar

⅓ cup + 2 tsp (90 ml) sparkling water (see Notes)

1¼ cups (150 g) all-purpose flour

¼ cup + 2 tbsp (45 g) fine corn flour

2 tsp (9 g) baking powder

⅛ tsp baking soda

⅛ tsp ground cardamom

⅛ tsp ground cinnamon

⅛ tsp sea salt

for serving

2 tsp (6 g) confectioners' sugar, optional

To make the Coffee Swirl, place the brown sugar, coconut sugar, espresso powder, cinnamon, walnuts and chocolate in a small bowl. Mix well to combine, then set aside.

Preheat the oven to 370°F (175°C), set an oven rack in the middle position and line an 8 x 4–inch (20 x 10–cm) loaf pan with parchment paper.

To make the Tea Cake, add the vegan butter, light brown sugar, oil and vanilla to a bowl. Cream until slightly fluffy with a hand or stand mixer, about 3 minutes. Set aside.

In a cup, mix the oat milk, apple cider vinegar and sparkling water to combine, then set aside.

In a separate bowl, mix the flours, baking powder, baking soda, cardamom, cinnamon and salt to combine.

Add one-third of the flour mixture and one-third of the liquid mixture to the creamed butter. Fold in gently, using a rubber spatula. Repeat the process until all the ingredients are combined. Be careful not to overmix the batter. Make sure you mix the batter with sparkling water mixture right before baking (see Notes).

Pour half of the batter into the prepared loaf pan. Sprinkle the Coffee Swirl mixture evenly over the batter, then pour in the remaining batter. Gently shake the pan so the batter is evenly distributed.

Bake for 35 minutes, or until a toothpick inserted comes out clean. Let the cake cool in the pan for 5 minutes, then transfer to a wire rack and let cool completely.

Dust with the confectioners' sugar, slice and serve.

This cake will keep for up to 4 days at room temperature, covered by a towel or stored in an airtight container.

notes

To powder any sugar, I use a powerful coffee grinder.

The sparkling water in this recipe **cannot** be substituted with still water. Sparkling water reacts with the other ingredients, making the final product aerated and light.

espresso marzipan raw truffles

These little espresso and marzipan truffles are quite addictive—the sweet, nutty almond flavor combines so beautifully with the aromatic coffee and vegan chocolate, I find it hard to resist them. To be honest, just writing this description makes me want to go into the kitchen and fix myself some truffles. Their texture is soft, chewy and slightly rough due to the ground almonds. Sometimes I like to use bitter almonds in the marzipan or, if I have it on hand, substitute the almond extract with some good old amaretto. I would double up on this recipe, as these will be gone so quickly.

Makes: 20 truffles | Raw, gluten-free, soy-free

espresso marzipan filling
2¾ cups (300 g) ground almonds

2 cups (240 g) confectioners' sugar

4 tsp (20 ml) almond extract

2 tsp (10 ml) rose water

4 tsp (8 g) espresso powder

6–8 tsp (30–40 ml) unsweetened almond milk

chocolate shell
8.5 oz (240 g) raw dark chocolate, or vegan dark chocolate, 75% cacao, chopped

1 tbsp (14 g) virgin coconut oil

To make the filling, place the ground almonds and sugar in a food processor. Process until well combined. Add the almond extract, rose water, espresso powder and almond milk. Process again until the mixture comes together. Divide the mixture into 20 equal parts (each will be about ½ ounce [30 g]) and shape into balls, then set aside on a plate.

Line a wide tray with parchment paper and set aside.

Prepare a double boiler. To do this, place a pot half filled with water on the stove and bring to a boil on a medium heat. On top of the pot, set a clean, heatproof bowl large enough so it does not touch the boiling water. (This technique is also called bain-marie, and it is used for transmitting a gentle heat. I recommend using it when melting chocolate as this ingredient can easily burn on high temperatures.)

Place the chocolate in the bowl and add the coconut oil. Mix well to combine and let the chocolate melt, then remove it from the heat and let it sit for 5 minutes. Alternatively, use my tempering method from Raw Lemon & Thyme Chocolate Bonbons recipe (page 81), for a more stable chocolate coating.

Using a fork, dip each marzipan ball into the melted chocolate. Transfer them to the parchment-lined tray and refrigerate for 30 minutes.

These marzipan truffles will keep well for up to 4 weeks, stored in an airtight container and refrigerated.

gluten-free poppy seed tea cake with raspberry cream cheese icing

Deliciously flavored with citrus, this cake is fresh and light. Little sparkles of poppy seeds embroider the crumb and give the cake a lovely crunch while enhancing its flavor with a slightly nutty and spicy taste. Made with a mix of corn, rice and oat flour, the cake develops other secondary nutty aromas that complement the overall cake, which I absolutely love. More often than not, gluten-free cakes tend to get dry, so a vegan cream cheese icing is here to give extra moisture to the cake, as well as to round things out with its creamy and tangy contrast. This is a truly joyful accompaniment to any hot drink, be it in the morning or afternoon!

Makes: 10–12 servings | Gluten-free, nut-free, soy-free

poppy seed cake

1¼ cups (150 g) fine corn flour

½ cup (75 g) white rice flour

½ cup (50 g) oat flour

¾ tsp xanthan gum (see Note)

2½ tbsp (25 g) poppy seeds

⅔ cup (135 g) light brown sugar

1½ tsp (7 g) baking powder

⅛ tsp baking soda

⅛ tsp sea salt

4½ tsp (25 ml) orange juice

¾ cup + 2 tbsp (210 ml) sweetened oat milk

¼ cup (60 ml) sunflower oil

Zest from 1 orange

Zest from ¼ lemon

2 tsp (10 ml) vanilla extract

raspberry cream cheese icing

1 tbsp (15 g) vegan butter, room temperature

3 tbsp (40 g) plain vegan cream cheese, cold

¼ cup (35 g) confectioners' sugar

Pinch of sea salt

¼ cup (35 g) fresh raspberries

1 tsp lemon juice

Zest from ½ orange, divided

1–2 tsp (5–10 ml) cold unsweetened oat milk, if needed

Preheat the oven to 370°F (175°C) and set an oven rack in the middle position. Lightly grease an 8 x 4–inch (20 x 10–cm) loaf pan with butter or nonstick cooking spray. Dust with flour, shaking off any excess.

To make the cake, mix the flours, xanthan gum, poppy seeds, light brown sugar, baking powder, baking soda and salt in a medium bowl.

In a separate bowl, mix the orange juice, oat milk, oil, citrus zest and vanilla well to combine. Pour the liquid mixture into the flour mixture and mix using a spatula or wooden spoon.

Pour the batter into the prepared loaf pan and bake for 30 to 35 minutes, until golden brown on top and a toothpick inserted in the middle comes out clean. Let the cake cool for 5 minutes in the pan, then transfer to a wire rack and let it cool completely before adding the cream cheese icing.

To make the icing, add the butter to a bowl. Give it a good mix using a wooden spatula until it becomes creamy. Add the vegan cream cheese and confectioners' sugar and mix vigorously, until the sugar is dissolved and the icing becomes smooth.

In a separate cup, smash the fresh raspberries and mix them with the lemon juice and half of the orange zest, keeping the other half for decorating the cake. Strain the raspberry mixture through a fine sieve then mix the puree with the vegan cream cheese mixture. Add the cold milk to make the icing more liquid, if needed.

Pour the icing over the completely cooled loaf cake and decorate with the reserved orange zest. Slice immediately, or refrigerate for 15 to 20 minutes to allow the icing to harden.

This cake will keep for 2 to 3 days, refrigerated, stored in an airtight container. Keep in mind that it tends to get drier after the first 2 days.

note

In this recipe, the xanthan gum helps thicken and hold the gluten-free baked good together. It also keeps it from becoming too crumbly. I do **not** recommend skipping this ingredient.

mixed nuts & amaranth snack bars

Packed with crunchy nuts and chewy fruits, these snack bars have long been a staple in my house. The earthy flavor of the pseudo-grain amaranth is beautifully paired with the rich date and almond base. Grated ginger and citrus give a bright note to these bars and they are perfect on the go, as a post-workout snack or to complement your breakfast.

I make these with whatever nuts or fruits I have on hand, and sometimes I like to use some puffed quinoa as well. As a bonus, they also keep for quite a long time in your fridge.

Makes: 6 bars | Gluten-free, soy-free, refined sugar-free

snack bars

2 cups (150 g) Medjool dates, pitted

2 tbsp (35 g) almond butter

1 tsp vanilla extract

Pinch of sea salt

2 tbsp (30 g) virgin coconut oil

1 tbsp (7 g) fresh ginger, shredded

Zest from 1 lemon

½ cup (60 g) dried cranberries

2 tbsp (20 g) raw almonds, chopped

2 tbsp (15 g) raw hazelnuts, chopped

2 tbsp (15 g) raw pistachios, chopped

⅓ cup (45 g) dried apricots, diced

2 tbsp (10 g) coconut flakes

⅓ cup (25 g) puffed amaranth (see Notes)

chocolate coating

1.5 oz (40 g) vegan dark chocolate, 75% cacao

Place the Medjool dates, almond butter, vanilla and sea salt in a high-speed blender. Blend well until creamy. Add the coconut oil and blend again until fully incorporated.

Transfer the mixture to a large bowl. Add the ginger, lemon zest, cranberries, chopped nuts, apricots, coconut flakes and puffed amaranth. Mix well using a wooden spoon. If you feel the mixture is hard to handle with a utensil, dive in with your hands and mix until the nuts, amaranth and dried fruits are well coated and incorporated.

Transfer the mixture to a 6½-inch (17-cm) square cake pan lined with cling film. Spread evenly and press down well using a spatula, in a flat layer. Refrigerate for at least 3 hours.

Transfer the chilled bars to a cutting board and cut in half. Slice each half into three bars. Arrange the bars on the cutting board.

Melt the chocolate in a double boiler. To make the double boiler, place a pot half filled with water on the stove and bring to a boil on medium heat. On top of the pot, add a clean, heatproof bowl large enough so it does not touch the boiling water. Place the chocolate in this bowl and stir until it melts.

When the chocolate has melted, drizzle it over the top of the bars. Refrigerate for 10 minutes before serving, so the chocolate is well set.

These bars will keep well for up to 3 weeks, refrigerated and stored into an airtight container.

notes

For this recipe, you can use any nuts, seeds and dried fruits you like.

You can find puffed amaranth online, or substitute puffed quinoa—or use a combination of the two.

rich & raw coconut chocolate bars

These coconut and chocolate bars are a vegan re-creation of the commercial confectionery Almond Joy™. Yet the pure ingredients in this version deliver a superior flavor and a beautiful, buttery texture that instantly captivates the appetite. They're also easy to prepare; just make sure you use a freshly opened batch of dried coconut, as this fruit tends to lose some of its aroma if left for too long in the cupboard.

Covered in a thick layer of dark chocolate, these glorious bars are simple, classic and delicious!

Makes: 10 bars | Raw, gluten-free, soy-free, refined sugar-free

bars

1¼ cups (130 g) dried shredded coconut

¾ cup (200 g) coconut butter (see Note)

½ cup (110 ml) agave nectar

3 tbsp (40 g) virgin coconut oil

1½ tsp (8 ml) vanilla extract

Pinch of sea salt

chocolate coating

5 oz (150 g) raw dark chocolate, or vegan dark chocolate, 75% cacao

Line a 6½-inch (17-cm) square cake pan with cling film.

Place the shredded coconut, coconut butter, agave nectar, coconut oil, vanilla and sea salt in a food processor and process until a fine meal is achieved and the mixture starts to become sticky.

Transfer the mixture to the lined pan and spread evenly. Press down with a rubber spatula to create a flat layer. Refrigerate for at least 1 hour. Cut the chilled bar in half. Slice each half into approximately five equal-sized bars. Set aside.

Line a tray with parchment paper and set aside.

Melt the chocolate in a double boiler. To make the double boiler, place a pot half filled with water on the stove and bring to a boil on medium heat. On top of the pot, add a clean, heatproof bowl large enough so it does not touch the boiling water. Place the chocolate in this bowl and stir until it melts.

Use two forks to dip each coconut bar into the melted chocolate, then transfer the bars to the prepared tray. Refrigerate for 30 minutes to set the chocolate before serving.

These bars will keep well for up to 3 to 4 weeks, refrigerated and stored in an airtight container.

note

You can find coconut butter in any health food store. You can also make your own coconut butter by simply blending unsweetened coconut flakes in a high-speed blender or food processor, until runny and creamy, 8 to 10 minutes.

booze

Vivid, funky and lip-smacking flavors are all gathered in this cheeky booze chapter. I've always been a fan of alcoholic desserts—I grew up with cakes that had cherries preserved in brandy, *baba au rhum*, or *betivana* (which literally translates to "the drunkard"). The latter used a mix of red wine and rum in the pastry cream, and it is a true delicacy.

During the development of this chapter, I've entertained myself by coming up with some of my favorite vegan bakes. These recipes are so good that I promise no one will even notice the missing eggs or dairy. All of the desserts are joyfully spiced with a hint of booze that just makes everything better.

Thinking of an easy but beautiful and delicious cake? The Caramelized Banana & Irish Cream Cake (page 140) is made from a simple spiced sponge topped with a flavorful, silky smooth caramelized banana and Irish cream frosting. For a breezy and vivid treat, I think the Strawberry, Prosecco & Lemon Curd Cake (page 143) is the best addition to any summer Sunday dinner. And if you want an innovative, vegan take on the classic pumpkin pie, I'm 100 percent confident that the Pumpkin & Bourbon Brûlée Tart (page 146) will conquer any pumpkin lover or non-pumpkin lover— it's that good!

caramelized banana & irish cream cake

Whenever I make cake, or any dessert for that matter, I put a lot of thought into the base: The crusts or sponges must always be so delicious that you'd want to eat them alone. This cake is so good, I sometimes make it into a loaf. It's warmly spiced with cloves and cinnamon and has a beautiful balance of caramel and banana flavors. It's rich and moist with a well-rounded flavor profile due to the previously cooked bananas. Yet you can be sure that the velvety Irish cream frosting makes all of this ten times better. You can go all fancy and decorate each slice (like I did) or you can simply spread all that chocolate ganache goodness over the whole cake, sprinkle it with a bit of crunchy almonds, slice and serve.

Makes: 10 servings | Soy-free

banana cake

¾ cup (170 ml) unsweetened oat milk

¼ cup + 2 tsp (70 ml) sunflower oil

¼ cup + 2 tsp (70 ml) vegan honey or maple syrup

¼ cup (60 g) muscovado sugar (see Notes)

¼ cup (50 g) light brown sugar

⅔ cup (100 g) ripe banana, mashed

¾ cup (100 g) white spelt flour

⅓ cup (50 g) all-purpose flour

⅛ tsp baking soda

1 tsp baking powder

¼ tsp ground Ceylon cinnamon (see Notes)

¼ tsp ground cloves

ganache

3 oz (70 g) full fat coconut milk, solids only

2 tbsp (30 g) light brown sugar

4 tsp (20 ml) maple syrup

⅛ tsp sea salt

3 oz (75 g) vegan dark chocolate, chopped

4 tsp (10 g) cornstarch

1 tbsp (15 ml) water

1 tsp coconut oil

½ cup (75 g) ripe banana, sliced

1 tsp vanilla extract

⅛ tsp ground cardamom

1½ tbsp (23 ml) Irish cream

Preheat the oven to 370°F (175°C), set an oven rack in the middle position and line an 8-inch (20-cm) square cake pan with parchment paper. Set aside.

To make the cake, mix the oat milk, oil, honey, sugars and mashed banana in a bowl.

In a separate bowl, whisk the spelt flour, all-purpose flour, baking soda, baking powder, cinnamon and cloves. Pour the milk and sugar mixture into the dry ingredients and fold in gently, being careful not to overmix.

Pour the batter into the prepared tin and bake for 25 to 30 minutes, or until the top is puffed and a toothpick inserted comes out clean. Let it cool completely in the pan on a wire rack.

To make the Ganache, place the coconut milk, sugar, maple syrup and salt in a saucepan and cook over medium heat until very hot, but not boiling, around 3 minutes. Reduce the heat to low and add the chopped chocolate. Stir a few times and let it melt completely.

Meanwhile, mix the cornstarch and water in a small cup until dissolved. Pour the cornstarch mixture over the melted chocolate. Stir it continuously and cook for 3 to 4 minutes on low heat, until it thickened. Set it aside to cool.

In a clean plan, heat the coconut oil over medium heat. Add the sliced banana and cook until it starts to get mushy, and is caramelized with brown patches, 3 to 5 minutes. Transfer the banana to a blender and pulse to make a smooth paste. Add the banana paste to the chocolate mixture along with the vanilla, cardamom and Irish cream. Mix well with a spoon. Let the chocolate ganache cool, then refrigerate for at least 2 hours or overnight.

(continued)

caramelized banana & irish cream cake (continued)

for serving

1–2 tbsp (7–14 g) toasted sliced almonds

To decorate, place the cake on a clean surface and trim the edges. Cut the cake in half then slice each half into ten rectangles, about 1 x 3½ inches (3 x 9 cm) each. Fill a piping bag with the chilled chocolate ganache, and using your preferred nozzle, decorate each slice of cake. Sprinkle each slice with toasted almonds.

Store the cake in an airtight container, for up to 4 days in the fridge.

Muscovado sugar can be purchased online, or you can substitute dark brown sugar.

Ceylon cinnamon is a Sri Lankan variety that has a lighter and sweeter flavor than Cassia cinnamon (the classic variety we find in stores). However, you can substitute the Ceylon with the same amount of classic cinnamon in this recipe.

To make this recipe quicker on the day you plan to serve it, prepare the ganache a day before. It needs to get chilled to set well, so it is better not to skip the refrigerating step.

If you want to make the cake faster or less fancy, you can make it into a sheet cake, skipping the slicing step and simply spread the ganache on top. Level using a spatula and sprinkle with toasted almonds, slice and serve.

strawberry, prosecco & lemon curd cake

Fresh strawberries, bubbly prosecco and smooth lemon curd create a divine combination of textures and flavors. The cake is made with part whole wheat flour, which gives a complementary, rustic dimension to the freshness of the toppings. I also kept the sponge quite thin because I find the ratio of the elements better balanced that way. And I know many of us prefer more of the creamy and fruity parts, especially in a fresh cake like this.

You can also switch the strawberries for other seasonal fruits like raspberry or peach as they pair incredibly well with the prosecco and the rest of the cake. As a final touch, sprinkle whatever you like (or have) on top of the strawberries; I went for shaved almonds and nigella seeds for a wonderful spicy pair to the whipped cream and strawberries.

Makes: 8 servings | Soy-free

lemon curd

⅓ cup + 1 tbsp (100 ml) sweetened oat milk

¼ cup (50 ml) vegan cooking cream (see page 10)

3 tbsp (35 g) caster/superfine sugar

Zest from 1 lemon

Small pinch of turmeric

Pinch of sea salt

2 tbsp (17 g) cornstarch

2 tsp (5 g) all-purpose flour

1½ tbsp (23 ml) water

1½ tbsp (20 g) vegan butter

1 tsp vanilla extract

2–3 tsp (10–15 ml) lemon juice

whole wheat cake

1 cup (125 g) all-purpose flour

½ cup (60 g) whole wheat flour

⅓ cup (85 g) light brown sugar

2 tsp (9 g) baking powder

¼ tsp baking soda

¼ tsp sea salt

1 oz (35 g) full-fat coconut milk, solids only, room temperature

¼ cup (50 ml) sweetened oat milk

2½ tbsp (35 g) vegan butter, melted

2 tsp (10 ml) vanilla extract

1 tbsp (15 ml) lemon juice

Zest from ½ lemon

To make the Lemon Curd, add the oat milk, cooking cream, sugar, lemon zest, turmeric and salt to a saucepan. Stir and cook on medium heat until it starts boiling, about 5 minutes.

In a small cup, combine the cornstarch, flour and water and mix until well dissolved. Turn the heat to low and pour the cornstarch mixture into the milk. Continue whisking and simmer on low for 8 to 10 minutes. When the mixture has thickened, remove the pan from the heat and stir in the vegan butter, vanilla and lemon juice. Mix well then place a cling film on the surface of the curd, so it does not form a skin on top, and let cool completely.

Preheat the oven to 370°F (175°C), set an oven rack in the middle position and line an 8-inch (21-cm) round cake pan with parchment paper.

To make the cake, in a large bowl, whisk the all-purpose flour, whole wheat flour, sugar, baking powder, baking soda and salt.

In a separate bowl, whisk the coconut milk, oat milk, melted vegan butter, vanilla, lemon juice and zest until homogenous. Pour the liquids into the flour mixture and fold using a spatula. Mix until it is just combined, making sure you don't overmix the batter.

Pour the batter into the prepared cake pan and bake for 30 minutes, until puffed and golden, and a toothpick inserted in the middle comes out clean. Let the cake cool for 5 minutes in the pan, then transfer to a wire rack and let it cool completely before decorating.

(continued)

strawberry, prosecco & lemon curd cake (continued)

macerated prosecco strawberries

2 cups (270 g) fresh strawberries, washed and cut in quarters

4 tsp (20 ml) agave syrup

3 tbsp (45 ml) prosecco

2 tsp (10 ml) lemon juice

1 tsp vanilla extract

for serving

1 tbsp (20 g) strawberry jam

5 oz (130 g) sweetened vegan whipped cream

1 tbsp (7 g) sliced almonds

½ tsp nigella seeds

To make the Macerated Prosecco Strawberries, place the strawberries, agave syrup, prosecco, lemon juice and vanilla in a medium bowl. Mix, then let everything macerate for at least 1 hour, at room temperature.

When the cake and curd are cooled, you can assemble the cake. Place the cake on a wide serving plate and brush it with the strawberry jam. Top it with the whipped cream and spread it around the surface, leaving 1 inch (2.5 cm) of the edges plain. On top of the whipped cream, spread the lemon curd using a spoon. Finally, strain the Macerated Prosecco Strawberries from the excess juice and place them on top of the curd, for a rustic effect. Sprinkle with the almonds and nigella seeds. Slice and serve.

This cake will keep for up to 2 days, covered or in a sealed container.

& bourbon brûlée tart

...tial autumn treat is beloved by everyone for obvious reasons. It's creamy, rich and spiced
...w of spices. For this recipe, I used my classic short crust recipe and by adding a touch of
...filling and syrup, I gave the pie an instant upgrade that I find perfect. To give it even more
...ed a butane torch to caramelize the top, creating an exquisite crunch. If you don't own a
butane torch, simply skip this part, as this tart comes served with a dollop of whipped cream and a drizzle
of maple and bourbon syrup that will ensure a show-stopping pie either way.

Makes: 8 servings | Nut-free, soy-free

short crust

1½ cups (200 g) all-purpose flour,
   plus more for rolling

6 tbsp (50 g) confectioners' sugar

Zest from 1 lemon

Pinch of sea salt

½ cup (115 g) vegan butter, cold
   and cubed

2 tbsp (30 ml) ice-cold sweetened
   oat milk

pumpkin filling

¾ cup + 2 tsp (200 ml) sweetened
   oat milk

⅓ cup + 1 tbsp (100 ml) vegan
   cooking cream (see page 10)

¼ cup (60 g) light brown sugar

Pinch of sea salt

3 tbsp (25 g) cornstarch

1¾ cups (15 oz [420 g]) pumpkin
   puree

1 tsp ground cinnamon

¼ tsp ground ginger

¼ tsp ground cloves

⅛ tsp ground nutmeg

1 tbsp (15 ml) maple syrup

1 tbsp (15 ml) bourbon whiskey

for serving

¼ cup (60 ml) maple syrup

2 tbsp (30 ml) bourbon whiskey

3 tbsp (35 g) caster/superfine sugar

4 oz (100 g) vegan whipped cream,
   sweetened

1 tsp ground nutmeg

To make the crust, add the flour, sugar, lemon zest and salt to the bowl of a food processor. Pulse to combine. Add the cubed butter to the flour mixture and pulse a few times, until just combined and the mixture resembles a coarse meal. Add the ice-cold milk and mix briefly, about 5 seconds, or until a soft dough starts to form. Transfer the dough on a floured working surface and shape it into a thick disk. Dust with flour on top and set aside.

Preheat the oven to 375°F (180°C) and set an oven rack in the middle position.

Roll the dough to a thin round, approximately 13 inches (32 cm). Lay the dough loosely into a 9½-inch (24-cm) fluted tart pan with a removable bottom. Press firmly against the pan so the finished edge is slightly higher than the pan. Trim the excess using a knife and freeze for 10 to 15 minutes.

Place pie weights (or dried beans) on top of the Short Crust to prevent it from rising. Bake the short crust for 20 minutes, or until the edges start to brown slightly. Leave the crust in the pan to cool completely.

To make the filling, add the milk to a saucepan and reserve 3 tablespoons (45 ml) of it in a cup. Add the cooking cream, sugar and salt to the saucepan and bring to a boil over medium heat. Mix the reserved milk with the cornstarch until well dissolved.

Add the cornstarch mixture to the boiling milk and cream, and cook on low for 7 to 8 minutes, stirring continuously so it doesn't stick to the pan, until thickened. Add the pumpkin puree, cinnamon, ginger, cloves and nutmeg and cook for another minute. Remove the pan from the heat and add the maple syrup and whiskey. Mix until well combined. Pour the hot filling into the pre-baked short crust and let cool completely at room temperature, then refrigerate for at least 4 hours or overnight.

When ready to serve, prepare the garnishes. In a small bowl with a pouring spout, mix the maple syrup and bourbon whiskey. Set aside.

Blot the top of the Pumpkin Filling dry with paper towels. Sprinkle the caster/superfine sugar all around the surface, then, using a butane torch, heat the sugar until melted and caramelized.

Slice the pumpkin tart and plate on serving plates: add a dollop of whipped cream on the side of each slice, and top with the maple and bourbon syrup. Sprinkle with a dash of ground nutmeg and enjoy! Keep the pumpkin tart refrigerated, for up to 5 days, in an airtight container.

raw apricot, vanilla & rum cake

This is another dessert that I kept on the permanent menu of our plant-based food business back in the day, and it became one of the favorites of our clients and our staff as well. The combo of tangy apricots, warm vanilla and aromatic chocolate hits the right spot, but the addition of a tiny bit of fragrant rum binds the other flavors together and results in a delicious, elevated dessert. What a revelation!

Makes: 10 servings | Raw, gluten-free, soy-free, refined sugar-free

chocolate base

¾ cup (80 g) raw cashews

¾ cup (90 g) coconut flour

1½ tbsp (15 g) hemp seeds

½ cup (65 g) Medjool dates, pitted

⅛ tsp sea salt

4 tbsp (20 g) cacao powder

1 tbsp (15 ml) agave nectar

1 tbsp (15 g) coconut oil

2 tsp (10 ml) vanilla extract

2 tsp (12 g) cacao nibs

apricot layer

1½ cups (250 g) pitted dried apricots

2 tbsp + 2 tsp (40 ml) lemon juice

1 tsp vanilla extract

2 tbsp (25 g) cacao butter, melted

2 tbsp (30 ml) virgin coconut oil, melted

rum & vanilla layer

1½ cups (175 g) raw cashews, soaked overnight

¼ cup (50 ml) unsweetened almond milk

⅓ cup (85 ml) agave nectar

4 tsp (20 ml) lemon juice

½ tsp lemon zest

⅛ tsp sea salt

3 tbsp (40 g) cacao butter, melted

1 tbsp (15 ml) good-quality rum

2 tsp (4 g) cacao powder

for serving

2 tsp (12 g) cacao nibs

2 tsp (2 g) dried rose petals

5–10 unsweetened coconut chips

To make the Chocolate Base, add the cashews, coconut flour, hemp seeds, Medjool dates and salt to a food processor and process until the mixture is fine crumbs. Add the cacao powder and pulse a few times until combined. Add the agave nectar, coconut oil, vanilla extract and cacao nibs and process a few seconds, until a sticky dough forms.

Line a 6½-inch (17-cm) square cake pan with cling film and place the crust mixture on the bottom. Spread evenly and use a rubber spatula or your hand to press it down into a neat, flat layer. Set aside.

To make the Apricot Layer, place the apricots, lemon juice and vanilla in a high-speed blender. Blend until smooth and creamy. Pour in the melted cacao butter and coconut oil and blend again until fully incorporated. Pour the filling on top of the nut base and spread evenly using a spatula. Place in the freezer and let it set for at least 15 minutes.

To make the Rum & Vanilla Layer, add the cashews, almond milk, agave nectar, lemon juice, zest and salt to a high-speed blender. Blend well until smooth and creamy. Pour in the melted cacao butter and rum and blend to fully combine.

Reserve 3 to 4 tablespoons (45 to 60 ml) of the rum and vanilla filling and transfer it to a small bowl. Add the cacao powder, mix to combine, then refrigerate. You will use this to decorate each slice.

Take the cake out of the freezer and pour the remaining rum and vanilla filling on top of the apricot layer. Spread evenly using a spatula and place it back into the freezer for at least 4 hours, or overnight.

When the cake is set, take it out of the freezer and let it sit for 10 minutes at room temperature.

Lift it out of the pan and place the cake on a cutting board. Trim the edges and cut the cake in half, then cut each half in five slices, as neatly as you can, using a sharp knife.

Add the reserved rum and vanilla filling to a piping bag. Using your favorite nozzle, decorate each slice with the chocolate filling. Sprinkle the top of each slice with the cacao nibs, rose petals and coconut chips.

This cake will keep well for up to 3 weeks in the freezer, in an airtight container. For a creamy but firm texture, defrost the cake for 1 to 2 hours in the refrigerator before serving.

tarte tatin with quince & cognac

Named after the Tatin sisters that invented this dessert, this tarte is technically an upside-down cake. It uses caramelized quinces in vegan butter and the overall taste is that of toffee and juicy, warm-flavored fruits. The flaky pastry gives a complementary texture to the soft and fleshy quince and caramel flavor. Personally, I love a lighter caramel, but if you like a stronger one, simply cook it for an additional minute. I also like to use a nice touch of alcohol in my tarte Tatin, so this version has cognac for a bit of punch and spice.

If you can't find quinces, or for a more classic version of the tarte Tatin, simply substitute Pink Lady apples.

Always serve it warm, with a scoop of vegan ice cream, a dollop of vegan whipped cream or vegan cooking cream. Divine!

Makes: 5–6 servings | Nut-free, soy-free

puff pastry

¾ cup (100 g) all-purpose flour, plus more for rolling

2 tbsp (15 g) confectioners' sugar

Pinch of sea salt

⅛ tsp baking soda

6½ tbsp (90 g) vegan butter, cold

2 tbsp + 2 tsp (40 ml) ice water

To make the Puff Pastry, add the flour, sugar, sea salt and baking soda to a bowl and mix. Grate the cold butter through the big holes of a grater, directly over the flour mixture. Use your fingertips to rub the butter into the flour mixture, though not as thoroughly as you might for a traditional pie dough, just enough so all the butter is covered by the flour mixture. Pour the ice water over the flour and butter and fold it in until it clumps together. If you need more moisture, add no more than 2 to 4 (10 to 20 ml) additional teaspoons.

Gently shape the dough into a 1-inch (2.5-cm)-thick square and wrap it in plastic wrap. Chill for at least 30 minutes. When chilled, place it on a floured surface and begin laminating the dough. Lamination is the process of folding and rolling the butter and dough over and over to create multiple layers. The lamination step is critical for creating the unique flaky texture of puff pastry. Roll out the dough and fold it in thirds. Sprinkle flour on top of the dough if necessary. Turn the dough 90 degrees and repeat the rolling, folding and rotating process two more times. Finally, roll the laminated dough into a 10-inch (25-cm) circle on the floured working surface. Keep turning the dough as you do this, to make sure it doesn't stick to the rolling surface.

Check the dough to make sure it's large enough to bake in an 8-inch (20-cm) cast-iron skillet (see Note). Move the crust onto a piece of parchment paper, cover with plastic wrap and refrigerate while you prepare the fruit filling.

Preheat the oven to 385°F (185°C) and set an oven rack in the middle position.

(continued)

tarte tatin with quince & cognac (continued)

filling

4 quinces (about 1 lb [460 g])

⅓ cup (80 g) caster/superfine sugar

¼ cup (50 ml) water

⅓ cup (70 g) vegan butter

1 tbsp (15 ml) lemon juice

Zest from ½ lemon

1½ tbsp (23 ml) cognac or brandy, plus more for deglazing

1 tbsp (15 ml) vanilla extract

for serving

6 scoops of vegan vanilla ice cream or vegan whipped cream

note

This tart bakes better in a cast-iron skillet, but if you don't have one, use a basic cake pan, without a detachable bottom.

To make the filling, peel and quarter the quinces. Use a small sharp knife to trim the hard cores and seeds from the center of each quarter, but don't worry about being too neat. If the quinces are too big, cut the quarters in half. Set aside.

Add the sugar and water to a saucepan and bring to a boil over medium heat. Cook for 5 to 7 minutes, until the caramel turns golden brown or slightly amber. Shake the pan from time to time, but don't stir with any utensil. If you like a more intense caramel flavor, let the mixture cook for an additional minute, until amber brown in color, but not darker than that, as the caramel will also be cooked in the oven. Keep in mind that the darker in color the caramel, the more bitter its aftertaste will be. Carefully pour the caramel into the bottom of a clean and dry 8-inch (20-cm) cast-iron skillet. Rotate the pan so the caramel covers the surface of the pan and be careful as the caramel will be extremely hot. Set aside to harden.

In a pan, cook the butter, lemon juice and lemon zest over medium–high heat until melted, about 3 minutes. Add the quinces and cook, stirring occasionally, for 12 to 15 minutes on medium heat, until slightly softer in texture. Remove the pan from the heat and add the cognac and vanilla and stir well into the released juice. Set aside for 5 minutes to cool slightly.

Spoon the quince mixture on top of the hardened caramel, in a concentric pattern. Squeeze in all the pieces. They will shrink slightly from baking and make room for any fruit slice that didn't fit completely at the beginning. Pour any excess juices from the cooked quince over the pan. Set aside.

Remove the dough from the refrigerator and place it on top of the quince. Brush off excess flour if there is any sticking to the dough. Tuck the edges under slightly, along the inside of the pan, using a spatula. To catch any leaking from the fruits when baking, place the skillet on a baking sheet and then place it into the preheated oven.

Bake for 20 to 25 minutes, or until the surface of the pastry is puffed, looks slightly brown, the edges are caramelized and the filling is bubbling. Allow the tart to cool for 5 to 10 minutes. Run a sharp knife along the inside edge of the pan. Place a plate or other serving dish on top of the pan and carefully but quickly flip over so the tart drops onto the plate. Be careful as the pan will still be hot. If there are any pieces of quince left behind in the pan or out of place, carefully put them back where they are supposed to be.

Add a little splash of cognac on the skillet pan and mix any remaining caramel sauce from the bottom of the cast iron, then gently brush the top of the quince slices with it. This step will give the tart a nice finish, both in look and taste. Slice and serve warm, with scoops of vanilla ice cream or vegan whipped cream.

This tart is better served fresh, on the same day, to enjoy the tender and flaky pastry.

wine-poached pears with cashew cream and seed brittle

This recipe creates an elegant dessert using fleshy and fragrant poached pears in spiced merlot with cinnamon, juniper and cardamom. The cashew cream adds some creaminess and body, while the spices bring some jazz to the plate. The crunchiness of the brittle is a fun and delectable addition—with nutty and caramel notes, this element should not be skipped.

Have a blast while plating these—you can serve them in elegant glasses, on round wide plates or in beautiful ceramic bowls.

Makes: 4 servings | Gluten-free, soy-free

cashew cream

1½ cups (150 g) raw cashews, soaked overnight

3 oz (90 g) full-fat coconut cream, solids only

2 tbsp + 2 tsp (40 ml) agave nectar

1½ tbsp (23 ml) lemon juice

½ tsp vanilla extract

⅛ tsp sea salt

2 tbsp (30 g) virgin coconut oil

1 tbsp (15 ml) unsweetened oat milk, optional

poached pears

3 cups (750 ml) red wine (Merlot or Shiraz)

¼ cup + 2 tbsp (100 g) caster/superfine sugar

2 cinnamon sticks

4 juniper pods

5 cloves

4 cardamom pods

2 strips orange peel

½ vanilla bean

4 medium-sized pears, washed and peeled (Bartlett or Bosc types are best for poaching)

To make the Cashew Cream, add the cashews, coconut cream, agave, lemon juice, vanilla and salt to a high-speed blender. Blend well until smooth and creamy. Add the coconut oil and blend again until fully incorporated. Transfer to an airtight container and refrigerate for at least 1 hour, until thickened.

Meanwhile, prepare the Poached Pears. Add the red wine, sugar, cinnamon sticks, juniper pods, cloves, cardamom pods and orange peel to a large pot. Cut the vanilla bean lengthwise and add it to the wine. Bring the mixture to a boil then reduce the heat to low.

Cut one or two pears in half, scoop out the core and keep the rest of the pears whole. Place the pears in the wine and let them poach over medium–low heat (simmering) for 20 to 25 minutes. Rotate the pears every 10 minutes to ensure they poach evenly on all sides, including the tops. When the pears have been poached, keep them upright in the poaching liquid, and remove the saucepan from the heat. Allow the pears to cool in the poaching liquid.

(continued)

wine-poached pears with cashew cream and seed brittle (continued)

seed brittle

⅓ cup (30 g) almonds, sliced and toasted

2 tsp (5 g) white sesame seeds, toasted

1 tsp black sesame seeds, toasted

1 tsp poppy seeds

1 tsp chia seeds

1 tsp Maldon flaky salt

½ cup (120 g) caster/superfine sugar

4 tsp (20 ml) water

½ tsp lemon juice

While the pears are cooling, prepare the Seed Brittle. Line half of a baking sheet with parchment paper. Sprinkle the almonds, sesame seeds, poppy seeds, chia seeds and salt on the parchment. Set aside.

In a saucepan, mix the sugar, water and lemon juice and bring to a boil over high heat, then reduce to heat to medium and allow the mixture to caramelize, until it is amber colored. To check if the sugar is well caramelized, scoop out a small amount of the caramel and pour it into a glass of cold water. If it hardens right away, it is ready. If not, continue boiling for an additional 1 to 2 minutes.

When caramelized, pour the brittle mixture onto the prepared pan with the seeds and almonds, spreading evenly with an offset metal spatula coated with cooking spray. Let cool completely and harden, then break into small- to medium-sized pieces before serving.

Before plating, check the Cashew Cream. If it has thickened in the refrigerator, whisk it vigorously and add the tablespoon (15 ml) of oat milk to loosen, if needed. Add about 3 tablespoons (45 ml) of the Cashew Cream to each plate. Top each plate with a Poached Pear and sprinkle with the Seed Brittle.

The Poached Pears can be served at room temperature or chilled and they will keep well for up to 2 days; however, they are best consumed on the same day.

Keep the brittle in an airtight container, at room temperature, for up to 3 days.

The cashew cream will keep well refrigerated, in an airtight container, for up to 3 days.

chestnut & cardamom rolls with rum syrup

These vegan rolls are soft and pillowy, and the sweet brioche is rolled up with a buttery and earthy chestnut filling and spiced with warm cardamom. The fragrant and funky rum syrup added at the end, as well as the muscovado, strategically placed on the bottom of the pan, makes these rolls a glorious, mouth-watering, sticky dessert. This recipe takes patience—not so much in preparation, but in awaiting the outcome, and yet the result is totally worth the wait!

I always use a sweetened chestnut spread, and if you're not familiar with it, I recommend you consider it—you can easily find it online or in any Italian or French food store under the names *crema di marroni* or *crème de marrons*. I promise you won't be disappointed; this spread is so good you'll eat it by the spoonful.

Makes: 10–12 servings | Soy-free

brioche

1 batch of Heavenly Poppy Seed & Raisin Babka Brioche Dough (page 119)

3 tbsp (42 g) muscovado sugar (see Note)

3 tbsp (40 g) vegan butter, cubed and at room temperature

1–2 tbsp (15–30 ml) sweetened almond milk

rum syrup

¼ cup (60 g) light brown sugar

¼ cup (60 ml) water

Peel from 1 lemon

Pinch of sea salt

2 tbsp (30 ml) good-quality rum

2 tsp (10 ml) vanilla extract

chestnut filling

1 cup (250 g) chestnut puree, sweetened (see recipe introduction)

½ cup (35 g) ground walnuts

2 tsp (4 g) ground cardamom

note

Muscovado sugar can be purchased online, or you can substitute dark brown sugar.

To make the Brioche Dough, follow the steps of the Heavenly Poppy Seed & Raisin Babka Brioche Dough. Grease a 9-inch (23-cm) round cake pan with butter. Sprinkle the muscovado sugar in the pan and place the cubed butter evenly across the bottom of the pan. This will ensure a nice caramelization on the bottom of your rolls. Set aside.

While the dough is proofing, prepare the Rum Syrup. Add the sugar, water, lemon peel and salt to a saucepan. Bring it to a boil on medium-high heat. Cook for 1 to 2 minutes then remove from the heat. Add the rum and vanilla and let cool completely. Set aside.

Place the proofed dough on a floured work surface and use a rolling pin to roll the dough out to an 11 x 20–inch (27 x 53–cm) rectangle. Gently spread the chestnut puree evenly on top of the rolled dough. Sprinkle it with the ground walnuts and cardamom. Roll up the dough tightly, then cut the log into two equal parts, then cut each part into five or six equal-sized rolls, using a sharp knife. Alternatively, use a clean thread to cut the dough log into perfect rolls. Slide it under your dough so that it's centered, wrap it around the top and pull tight in one quick motion. The floss/thread should cut cleanly and easily through the dough.

Place the rolls into the prepared cake pan. Let proof for 1 hour at room temperature or in a warm spot, covered with a loose, clean plastic bag.

Preheat the oven to 370°F (175°C) and set an oven rack in the middle position.

When the rolls are puffed, brush them gently with the almond milk. Bake for 20 minutes, then lower the oven temperature to 340°F (160°C). Bake for an additional 25 minutes. Take the rolls out of the oven and quickly pour the Rum Syrup over them. Let it absorb at room temperature, covered for at least 15 minutes, before serving.

These rolls will keep well for up to 3 days, in an airtight container, at room temperature. Slightly reheat the rolls in a microwave before serving.

plum & prosecco sorbet with crunchy nougatine

The first days of fall welcome me into the kitchen with sweet, fragrant plums. Paired with a crunchy, nutty and earthy nougatine, this plum sorbet is a true delicacy. The riper the plums are the better, but I've made this with medium-ripe plums and it works well then, too. That's because throughout the cooking process, the plums release their aromatic flavor profile, deep color and sweetness.

Makes: 4 servings | Gluten-free, soy-free

plum & prosecco sorbet

15 oz (410 g) plums, well ripened
   (Damson variety works best)
⅓ cup (70 g) cane sugar
¼ cup (50 ml) water
1 cinnamon stick
Pinch of sea salt
2 tsp (10 ml) vanilla extract
Juice from ½ lemon
2–3 tbsp (30–45 ml) prosecco

sage nougatine

½ cup 100 g white sugar
¼ cup (60 ml) cold water
Small pinch of sea salt
1 cup (100 g) finely chopped mixed
   toasted nuts (walnuts, cashews,
   almonds)
6 small to medium fresh sage
   leaves, finely sliced

Preheat the oven to 375°F (180°C) and set an oven rack in the middle position.

To make the sorbet, wash and halve the plums, taking out the pit. Place the plums in a single layer on a deep baking sheet. Bake for 15 to 17 minutes or until they are soft and the juice is bubbling. Remove from the oven and let them cool completely.

Meanwhile, in a saucepan, mix the cane sugar, water, cinnamon stick and salt over medium heat and bring to a boil. Simmer for 5 minutes, then turn off the heat. Let cool completely, with the cinnamon stick still in the liquid.

When the plums and syrup are cool, remove the cinnamon stick and place them in a high-speed blender. Add the vanilla, lemon juice and prosecco and blend well, until creamy. Strain through a sieve into a clean bowl.

If you have an ice cream maker, add the mixture and process according to the manufacturer's instructions. If you don't have one, use the following tip: Pour the mixture into a gallon-sized freezer bag. Lay it flat on a tray and freeze it until solid, about 2 to 3 hours. When frozen, break the mixture into large chunks and blend again until smooth, working in batches if necessary. Transfer to a container and freeze until firm, about 3 hours or overnight. This technique will help break down ice crystals formed and give the sorbet a softer and creamier texture.

To make the nougatine, line a baking tray with parchment paper and spray with oil. Set aside.

Place the sugar and water in a saucepan, mix with a spoon and place it over medium heat. Bring to a boil and don't mix the sugar. Reduce the heat to low and allow it to cook, undisturbed, for 6 to 8 minutes, until it turns a light brown color. Add the salt, chopped nuts and sage and stir very quickly until everything is well coated. Remove the pan from the heat and quickly transfer the mixture to the prepared tray, spreading evenly and working quickly with an oiled spoon. Let the mixture harden at room temperature, about 10 minutes. When set and hard, break the nougatine into irregular pieces.

Plate the sorbet in serving cups, placing approximately 1½ scoops in each cup. Add a piece of nougatine on top, inserted vertically to give the composition a nice tall structure.

Keep the sorbet in an airtight container in the freezer for up to 3 to 4 weeks. The nougatine can be stored in an airtight container for 2 to 3 days, but it will lose some of its crunch due to humidity. It is best enjoyed on the same day.

boozy cherry truffles

Covered in crackling vegan chocolate, these Boozy Cherry Truffles have a dense and decadent dark chocolate and hazelnut filling. They are filled with alcohol-soaked fleshy fruits, and I find this timeless combination of cherries and chocolate to be perfect for any occasion.

The flavor of cacao butter and hazelnut gives these truffles a spectacular taste and texture. They literally melt in your mouth and are the definition of delight.

Making them is not complicated at all—start by blending the hazelnut and cocoa filling, freeze to set, shape into truffles then cover with the melted chocolate. To make them more quickly the day you plan to serve them, start the cherries the night before and let them infuse with the cognac and spices overnight.

Makes: 14 servings | Raw, gluten-free, soy-free, refined sugar-free

boozy cherries

28 pitted sour cherries, frozen or fresh

1 tbsp (15 ml) cognac or brandy

1 tbsp (15 ml) maple syrup

Pinch of ground cloves

chocolate truffles

½ cup (65 g) raw hazelnuts

3 tbsp (35 g) coconut sugar

¼ cup (55 ml) sweetened almond milk

¼ cup (25 g) cacao powder

¼ cup (60 ml) maple syrup

2 tsp (10 ml) vanilla extract

⅛ tsp sea salt

1 tbsp (20 g) cacao butter, melted

coating

3 oz (80 g) raw dark chocolate, or vegan dark chocolate, 75% cacao

2 tbsp (24 g) coconut sugar

2–3 tbsp (11–16 g) cacao powder

To prepare the Boozy Cherries, add the cherries, cognac, maple syrup and ground cloves to a bowl. Give it a mix and let the cherries sit in alcohol for at least 3 hours, or overnight.

To make the truffles, add the raw hazelnuts to a high-speed blender and blend until very fine and a paste starts to form. Add the coconut sugar and almond milk and blend again, about 1 minute, until creamy and smooth. Add the cacao powder, maple syrup, vanilla and salt and blend again to fully incorporate. Finally, pour the melted butter in slowly while the blender is working to emulsify the batter. Transfer the mixture to a wide plate, cover it with cling film and spread it out. Freeze for at least 2 hours.

Strain the cherries and set aside.

When ready to assemble the truffles, take the truffle batter out of the freezer and divide it into fourteen equal pieces. Shape each into a ball, then flatten with your fingers to form a disk. Place two cherries in the middle of each piece, then enclose the cherries with the truffle batter. Roll in your hands, working fast as they tend to melt quickly. Repeat with all the truffle batter.

To coat the truffles, cover a baking tray with cling film. Set aside. Melt the raw dark chocolate on a double boiler, then refrigerate for 10 minutes. To make the double boiler, place a pot half filled with water on the stove and bring to a boil on a medium heat. On top of the pot, add a clean heatproof bowl large enough so it does not touch the boiling water. Place the chocolate in this bowl and stir until melted.

Using a fork, dip the truffles into the melted chocolate, working with two or three at a time. Transfer the coated truffles to the cling film–lined baking tray. Roll some of the truffles immediately in the coconut sugar, so it will stick better to the chocolate. Transfer to a serving plate.

Allow the rest of the truffles to set, then roll some of the truffles in the cacao powder. You can keep the remaining truffles with just the chocolate coating. This way you will get variations of interesting coatings. Place them all on a serving plate and refrigerate the leftovers.

These truffles will keep for up to 4 days in an airtight container, refrigerated, or up to 3 weeks in the freezer.

irish cream & earl grey semifreddo

Here is another easy and quick dessert that demands little in terms of preparation, but delivers with its flavor. I am a tea enthusiast and I find the pleasant and robust flavor of Earl Grey fascinating in food. It pairs wonderfully with the vegan almond Irish cream and this indulging frozen dessert makes a great end to any meal. This recipe uses cashews and vegan cooking cream as a base, so the semifreddo results in a rich and soft cream.

Makes: 6–8 servings | Raw, gluten-free, soy-free, refined sugar-free

3 tbsp (15 g) Earl Grey loose-leaf tea

⅓ cup + 1 tbsp (100 ml) boiling water

¾ cup (90 g) raw cashews, soaked overnight

3 tbsp (50 ml) vegan cooking cream (see page 10)

4 oz (110 g) full-fat coconut milk, solids only

¼ cup (60 ml) maple syrup

⅛ tsp sea salt

2 tsp (10 ml) vanilla extract

1–2 tbsp (15–30 ml) vegan Irish cream, such as Baileys Almande™

2 oz (60 g) raw dark chocolate, or vegan dark chocolate, 65% cacao, divided

¼ cup (35 g) vegan powdered coconut milk

Place the tea in a cup and pour the boiling water over it. Leave it to infuse for 10 minutes.

Place the cashews in a high-speed blender. Add the cooking cream, coconut milk, maple syrup, salt, vanilla and vegan Irish cream. Blend well until smooth and creamy.

Strain the tea, and measure out ¼ cup (50 ml) of black tea. Set aside.

Measure out 1 cup (230 ml) of the mixture from the blender and pour it into a clean bowl. Finely chop half of the dark chocolate, then add it to the cream mixture in the bowl. Refrigerate.

Pour the strained black tea into the remaining cream in the blender. Add the powdered coconut milk and blend again until combined.

Line a 3 x 7–inch (8 x 17–cm) container with cling film. Pour the Earl Grey mixture into the container and freeze for 1 hour. Remove the frozen mixture and spread the refrigerated chocolate cream on top. Freeze one more time, for at least 3 hours or overnight.

Before serving, plate the semifreddo and let it defrost in the refrigerator for about 15 minutes. Shave the remaining chocolate and sprinkle it on top of the semifreddo. Slice and serve right away.

The semifreddo will keep well in the freezer for up to 3 weeks in an airtight container.

acknowledgments

Writing this cookbook was so much harder than I thought, yet I am incredibly proud of this debut, and grateful to everyone involved:

To the countless home cooks, bakers, chefs and authors who came before me and enriched my knowledge and skills, thank you. You sparked the curiosity in me and I will be forever grateful for all of your work.

Thank you to Arielle Smolin, who first approached me, believed in my vision and took a chance with me. I am grateful to Caitlin and Sarah, my editors who kindly understood me and the creative process a book demands. Thank you for giving me the time I needed and of course, thank you for bringing this book to life. Thank you to Meg Baskis for the gorgeous design and for honoring my ideas, too. Thank you to Charlotte, Jamie, Katelynn, William and everyone at Page Street Publishing for being so kind, and being the most professional team I have worked with.

My warmest thanks to my mother, Melania, and father, Florin, who never ceased to support my life choices. I would have never been here without your tremendous and caring love. Thank you both, and thank you to my extended family who made loving food a family imperative.

Thank you to my paternal grandmother, Marta, for our random conversations over the phone that relaxed me on my most difficult days. To my grandfather, Teodor, who's such a great storyteller and filled my soul with food memories from his life.

I am forever grateful to my sister, Diana. Thank you for making me laugh in my moments of despair or for no reason at all. I honestly don't know how to declare the depths of my appreciation and love for you. All the words fall flat in comparison to your support, love and warmth.

Andrada, thank you for believing in me right from day zero when I started cooking with a blender on my laptop table and between our uni projects. Thank you for your pure love and for being the quiet force that you are.

Merci mille fois Iulia, for cheering and supporting with every step. Thank you for always giving me thoughtful advice and continually celebrating my successes and shouting about them far and wide. Thank you both for always treating my passion for cooking seriously and respectfully. I am sincerely grateful for that and I love you both.

Thank you to my joyful friends Germina, Rita and Theo for your positivity, cheerfulness and for your sense of humor about all things. Your friendship and encouragement mean a lot to me.

Thank you to my epic husband, Andrei. Thank you for tasting every recipe in this book and beyond, and giving me sharp and honest feedback. Thank you for all the countless dishes washed and all the runs to Mega you did for me. I would've had a total mental breakdown if not for your help! I am forever grateful for the pasta and sandwiches you made for me but I am especially grateful for the warmth and care you showed me when I was not feeling well from too much sugar. Thank you for your morning massages, for editing my crazy rough manuscript, for making me laugh and always loving me deeply.

And finally, a tremendous thank you to all my readers and Instagram followers. Thank you for your invaluable support, feedback and enthusiasm, and for making (and presumably liking) the recipes I put into the world. You are the first reason this book is possible. Thank you from the bottom of my heart.

about the author

Ana Rusu is the recipe developer, food photographer and stylist behind the blog Herbs & Roots (now ana-rusu.com). An artist turned food stylist, she's known for her striking aesthetic and creative, flavor-forward style of cooking. She was born and raised in a small city in Romania and she's been working professionally in the food industry since 2014.

Half self-taught, half trained at Matthew Kenney's culinary academy, Ana began her education early on, in the kitchen of her childhood home, where she helped and observed her grandmother—the greatest cook and baker she could possibly learn from. Now a freelance vegan chef, Ana develops recipes and works as a food photographer for brands across the world.

index

A

Almond & Cornmeal Bundt Cake with Orange Syrup, 89
almonds
Almond & Cornmeal Bundt Cake with Orange Syrup, 89
Black Sesame Seeds & Matcha Cookies, 122
Carrot Cake with Homemade Carrot Jam, 101
Chocolate, Chili & Sea Salt Cookies, 20
Crisp & Gooey Gingersnap Cookies, 96
Crispy & Flaky Dried Fruit Biscuits, 65
Espresso Marzipan Raw Truffles, 130
Flourless Chocolate Torte with Sticky Ganache, 33–34
Mixed Nuts & Amaranth Snack Bars, 134
Pâte Sucrée, 68
Pecan & Plum Crescents, 126
Rustic Peach & Blackberry Galette, 55–56
Sage Nougatine, 159
Seed Brittle, 155
Star Anise & Pecan Biscotti, 105
Sticky Date Cake, 27–29
Vanilla Sugar Cookies, 46
Amaranth Snack Bars, Mixed Nuts &, 134
Apple Kataifi with Vegan Whipped Cream, 61
apricots, dried
Crispy & Flaky Dried Fruit Biscuits, 65
Mixed Nuts & Amaranth Snack Bars, 134
Raw Apricot, Vanilla & Rum Cake, 148
Aquafaba Meringues, 49
Aquafaba Pavlova, 62

B

Banana & Irish Cream Cake, Caramelized, 140
Bergamot & Olive Oil Yogurt Sorbet, 85
Black Sesame Seeds & Matcha Cookies, 122

blackberries
Blackberry & Lavender Ice Cream Sandwiches, 46
Rustic Peach & Blackberry Galette, 55–56
blueberries
Blueberry Compote, 110
Decadent Blueberry Pavlova, 62
Boozy Cherry Truffles, 160
bourbon whiskey
Pecan & Plum Crescents, 126
Pumpkin & Bourbon Brûlée Tart, 146

C

cakes
Almond & Cornmeal Bundt Cake, 89
Caramelized Banana & Irish Cream Cake, 140–142
Carrot Cake with Homemade Carrot Jam, 101–102
Chantilly & Diplomat Cream with Tropical Fruit Cake, 42
Cherry & Chocolate Lamingtons, 35–36
Chocolate, Cardamom & Tahini Cupcakes, 92
Chocolate Cake with Blackcurrant Jam, 14–16
Classic Lemon Butter Loaf Cake, 74
Coffee, Cinnamon & Walnut Tea Cake, 129
Dulce de Leche Bundt Cake, 17–19
Festive Lime & Coconut Cake, 71–73
Flourless Chocolate Torte, 33–34
Gluten-Free Poppy Seed Tea Cake, 133
Gluten-Free Upside-Down Sour Cherry Cake, 51–52
Orange & Cinnamon Phyllo Cake, 77
Raw Apricot, Vanilla & Rum Cake, 148
Salted Caramel Boston Pie, 24–26
Six-Layer Mocha Cake, 116–118
Spiced Vegan Honey & Semolina Cake, 99–100
Sticky Date Cake, 27–29
Strawberry, Prosecco & Lemon Curd Cake, 143–145
Wild Berries & Cinnamon Streusel Muffins, 109
Caramelized Banana & Irish Cream Cake, 140–142
Carrot Cake with Homemade Carrot Jam, 101–102

Carrot Jam, 101
cashews
Blackberry & Lavender Ice Cream Sandwiches, 46
Cashew Cream, 153
Irish Cream & Earl Grey Semifreddo, 163
Lemon & Thyme Filling, 81
Lime Cream, Ginger Nuts & Cola Gel Verrines, 78
Raw Apricot, Vanilla & Rum Cake, 148
Raw Vanilla & Lime Cheesecake Tart, 86
Sage Nougatine, 159
Wine-Poached Pears with Cashew Cream and Seed Brittle, 153
World's Best Raw Caramel Bars, 23
Chantilly & Diplomat Cream with Tropical Fruit Cake, 42
cherries, sour
Boozy Cherry Truffles, 160
Gluten-Free Upside-Down Sour Cherry Cake with Crème Anglaise, 51
Cherry & Chocolate Lamingtons, 35–36
Chestnut & Cardamom Rolls with Rum Syrup, 156
Chocolate, Cardamom & Tahini Cupcakes, 92
Chocolate, Chili & Sea Salt Cookies, 20
Chocolate Brownies, Fudgy Double, 30
Chocolate Cake with Blackcurrant Jam, 14–16
Chocolate Frosting, 14
Chocolate Ganache, 26, 33, 118
Chocolate Glaze, 19, 36
Chocolate Mousse with Spicy Mango, 39
Classic Lemon Butter Loaf Cake, 74
cocoa/cacao powder
Boozy Cherry Truffles, 160
Chocolate, Cardamom & Tahini Cupcakes, 92
Chocolate Cake with Blackcurrant Jam, 14
Dark Chocolate Mousse with Spicy Mango, 39
Flourless Chocolate Torte with Sticky Ganache, 33–34
Fudgy Double Chocolate Brownies, 30
Raw Lemon & Thyme Chocolate Bonbons, 81
Sticky Date Cake, 27

coconut
  Cherry & Chocolate Lamingtons, 35–36
  Festive Lime & Coconut Cake, 71
  Lime Cream, Ginger Nuts & Cola Gel Verrines, 78
  Mixed Nuts & Amaranth Snack Bars, 134
  Rich & Raw Coconut Chocolate Bars, 137
  World's Best Raw Caramel Bars, 23
Coconut Dulce de Leche, 17
Coffee, Cinnamon & Walnut Tea Cake, 129
Coffee Parfait with Boba Pearls & Biscotti, 125
cognac
  Boozy Cherry Truffles, 160
  Tarte Tatin with Quince & Cognac, 152
cookies and bars
  Black Sesame Seeds & Matcha Cookies, 122
  Chocolate, Chili & Sea Salt Cookies, 20
  Crisp & Gooey Gingersnap Cookies, 96
  Crispy & Flaky Dried Fruit Biscuits, 65
  Fudgy Double Chocolate Brownies, 30
  Gluten-Free Pumpkin & White Chocolate Oat Bars, 113
  Mixed Nuts & Amaranth Snack Bars, 134
  Pecan & Plum Crescents, 126
  Star Anise & Pecan Biscotti, 105
  Vanilla Sugar Cookies, 46
  World's Best Raw Caramel Bars, 23
cranberries, dried
  Crispy & Flaky Dried Fruit Biscuits, 65
  Mixed Nuts & Amaranth Snack Bars, 134
Crème Anglaise, 51
Crisp & Gooey Gingersnap Cookies, 96
Crispy & Flaky Dried Fruit Biscuits, 65
Custard Filling, 26

D
Dark Chocolate Mousse with Spicy Mango, 39
dates, Medjool
  Mixed Nuts & Amaranth Snack Bars, 134

Raw Apricot, Vanilla & Rum Cake, 148
Sticky Date Cake, 27–29
World's Best Raw Caramel Bars, 23
Decadent Blueberry Pavlova, 62
desserts
  Apple Kataifi with Vegan Whipped Cream, 61
  Coffee Parfait with Boba Pearls & Biscotti, 125
  Dark Chocolate Mousse with Spicy Mango, 39
  Decadent Blueberry Pavlova, 62
  Light & Fresh Eton Mess, 49–50
  Lime Cream, Ginger Nuts & Cola Gel Verrines, 78
  Matcha Rice Pudding with Blueberry Compote, 110
  Pumpkin Mousse & Cookie Crumb Parfait, 95
  Romanian Plum Dumplings, 45
  Saffron Panna Cotta with Rose & Raspberry Coulis, 106
  Wine-Poached Pears with Cashew Cream and Seed Brittle, 153–155
Dulce de Leche Bundt Cake with Chocolate Glaze, 17–19

E
Espresso Marzipan Raw Truffles, 130

F
Festive Lime & Coconut Cake, 71–73
Flourless Chocolate Torte with Sticky Ganache, 33–34
frostings
  Chocolate Frosting, 14
  Chocolate Ganache, 26, 33, 118
  Chocolate Glaze, 19, 36
  classic sugar icing, 74
  Mocha Buttercream, 118
  Pumpkin Frosting, 113
  Raspberry Cream Cheese Icing, 133
  Tahini Buttercream, 92
  Vegan Cream Cheese Frosting, 102
frozen desserts
  Bergamot & Olive Oil Yogurt Sorbet, 85
  Blackberry & Lavender Ice Cream Sandwiches, 46
  Irish Cream & Earl Grey Semifreddo, 163
  Mango, Lime & Cucumber Ice Pops, 82

Plum & Prosecco Sorbet with Crunchy Nougatine, 159
Fudgy Double Chocolate Brownies, 30

G
Gluten-Free Poppy Seed Tea Cake with Raspberry Cream Cheese Icing, 133
Gluten-Free Pumpkin & White Chocolate Oat Bars, 113
Gluten-Free Upside-Down Sour Cherry Cake with Crème Anglaise, 51–52

H
hazelnuts
  Boozy Cherry Truffles, 160
  Mixed Nuts & Amaranth Snack Bars, 134
  Raw Vanilla & Lime Cheesecake Tart, 86
Heavenly Poppy Seed & Raisin Babka, 119–121

I
Irish Cream
  Caramelized Banana & Irish Cream Cake, 140
  Irish Cream & Earl Grey Semifreddo, 163

L
Lavender Ice Cream, Blackberry &, 46
Lemon & Thyme Filling, 81
Lemon Butter Loaf Cake, Classic, 74
Lemon Curd, 143
Lemon Posset Tart with Raspberry and Whipped Cream, 68–70
Light & Fresh Eton Mess, 49–50
Lime & Coconut Cake, Festive, 71–73
Lime Coconut Filling, 73
Lime Cream, Ginger Nuts & Cola Gel Verrines, 78

M
Macerated Prosecco Strawberries, 145
Macerated Strawberries, 50
Mango, Lime & Cucumber Ice Pops, 82
mangos
  Chantilly & Diplomat Cream with Tropical Fruit Cake, 42
  Dark Chocolate Mousse with Spicy Mango, 39
  Mango, Lime & Cucumber Ice Pops, 82

Maple & Citrus Syrup, 61
Matcha Rice Pudding with Blueberry
Compote, 110
Mixed Nuts & Amaranth Snack Bars,
134
Mocha Buttercream, 118

O
Oat Bars, Gluten-Free Pumpkin &
White Chocolate, 113
oranges
Almond & Cornmeal Bundt Cake
with Orange Syrup, 89
Chantilly & Diplomat Cream with
Tropical Fruit Cake, 42
Crispy & Flaky Dried Fruit Biscuits,
65
Gluten-Free Poppy Seed Tea
Cake with Raspberry Cream
Cheese Icing, 133
Gluten-Free Upside-Down Sour
Cherry Cake with Crème
Anglaise, 51
Maple & Citrus Syrup, 61
Orange & Cinnamon Phyllo Cake,
77
Orange Syrup, 89
Poppy Seed Filling, 121
Raspberry Cream Cheese Icing,
133

P
Pâte Sucrée, 68
Peach & Blackberry Galette, 55–56
Pears with Cashew Cream and Seed
Brittle, Wine-Poached, 153
Pecan & Plum Crescents, 126
pecans
Ginger Nuts, 78
Pecan & Plum Crescents, 126
Pumpkin Mousse & Cookie Crumb
Parfait, 95
Star Anise & Pecan Biscotti, 105
Perfectly Flaky Mixed Summer Fruit
Pie, 57–58
Phyllo Cake, Orange & Cinnamon, 77
pies and tarts
Lemon Posset Tart with Raspberry
and Whipped Cream, 68–70
Perfectly Flaky Mixed Summer
Fruit Pie, 57–58
Pumpkin & Bourbon Brûlée Tart,
146

Raw Vanilla & Lime Cheesecake
Tart, 86
Rustic Peach & Blackberry Galette,
55–56
Plum & Prosecco Sorbet with Crunchy
Nougatine, 159
plums
Pecan & Plum Crescents, 126
Plum & Prosecco Sorbet with
Crunchy Nougatine, 159
Plum Filling, 45
Poppy Seed & Raisin Babka,
Heavenly, 119–121
Poppy Seed Filling, 121
Poppy Seed Tea Cake, Gluten-Free,
133
prosecco
Macerated Prosecco Strawberries,
145
Plum & Prosecco Sorbet with
Crunchy Nougatine, 159
Pumpkin & Bourbon Brûlée Tart, 146
Pumpkin Custard, 95
Pumpkin Frosting, 113
Pumpkin Mousse & Cookie Crumb
Parfait, 95

R
raspberries
Decadent Blueberry Pavlova, 62
Lemon Posset Tart with Raspberry
and Whipped Cream, 68
Light & Fresh Eton Mess, 49–50
Raspberry Cream Cheese Icing,
133
Rose & Raspberry Coulis, 106
Raw Apricot, Vanilla & Rum Cake, 148
Raw Lemon & Thyme Chocolate
Bonbons, 81
Raw Vanilla & Lime Cheesecake Tart,
86
Rice Pudding with Blueberry
Compote, Matcha, 110
Rich & Raw Coconut Chocolate Bars,
137
Romanian Plum Dumplings, 45
Rose & Raspberry Coulis, 106
rum
Chestnut & Cardamom Rolls with
Rum Syrup, 156
Raw Apricot, Vanilla & Rum Cake,
148
Rustic Peach & Blackberry Galette,
55–56

S
Saffron Panna Cotta with Rose &
Raspberry Coulis, 106
Sage Nougatine, 159
Salted Caramel Boston Pie, 24–26
Seed Brittle, 155
Semolina Custard Cream, 99
Six-Layer Mocha Cake, 116–118
Spiced Vegan Honey & Semolina
Cake, 99–100
spinach leaves
Lime Cream, Ginger Nuts & Cola
Gel Verrines, 78
Raw Vanilla & Lime Cheesecake
Tart, 86
Star Anise & Pecan Biscotti, 105
Sticky Date Cake with Toffee &
Vanilla Ice Cream, 27–29
strawberries
Light & Fresh Eton Mess, 49–50
Macerated Prosecco Strawberries,
145
Strawberry, Prosecco & Lemon
Curd Cake, 143–145

T
Tahini Buttercream, 92
Tarte Tatin with Quince & Cognac,
150–152
Toffee Sauce, 27

V
Vanilla Custard, 42
Vanilla Sugar Cookies, 46
Vanilla-Lime Filling, 86
Vegan Cream Cheese Frosting, 102

W
walnuts
Carrot Cake with Homemade
Carrot Jam, 101
Chestnut & Cardamom Rolls with
Rum Syrup, 156
Coffee, Cinnamon & Walnut Tea
Cake, 129
Sage Nougatine, 159
Wild Berries & Cinnamon Streusel
Muffins, 109
Wine-Poached Pears with Cashew
Cream and Seed Brittle, 153–155
World's Best Raw Caramel Bars, 23